MW00891983

The Highly Sensitive Person's Growth Guide

How To Feel Empowered in an
Overstimulated World

Damian Blair

Disclaimer

No part of this publication may be reproduced, stored in a retrieval system or transmitted in any form or by any means, electronic, mechanical, photocopying, recording, scanning or otherwise except as permitted under Sections 107 or 108 of the 1976 United States Copyright Act, without the prior written permission of the publisher.

While every precaution has been taken in the preparation of this book, the publisher assumes no responsibility for errors or omissions, or for damages resulting from the use of the information contained herein.

This book is for entertainment and informational purposes only. The views expressed are those of the author alone and should not be taken as expert instruction or commands. The reader is responsible for his or her own actions. Neither the author nor the publisher assumes any responsibility or liability whatsoever on behalf of the purchaser or reader of these materials. The reader is responsible for their own use of any products or methods mentioned in this publication.

This book may include information about products and equipment offered by third parties. As such, the author does not assume responsibility or liability for any third party products or opinions. Third party product manufacturers have not sanctioned this book, nor does the author receive any compensation from said manufacturers for sharing information regarding their products.

The Highly Sensitive Person's Growth Guide
First edition. October 4, 2021
Copyright © 2021 Damian Blair

Table of Contents

4

Introduction

Do you get easily overwhelmed when confronted with crowded places and chaotic environments? Do you have a stronger emotional reaction to environmental noise than those around you?

Highly sensitive people (or HSPs for short) frequently experience the urge to withdraw from overstimulating environments, often demanding a safe haven where they can be alone and ground their reactions in order to function properly. If you fall into this category may feel alone due to the fact that you are unable to enjoy, or even tolerate, certain activities in the same way others do.

While your aversions may be difficult to accept at times, they are merely the result of your genetic makeup and can be successfully managed.

During my tenure as therapist, I studied the highly sensitive trait in many of my clients. Having witnessed their personal struggles, I decide to write this book as a way to improve the life of individuals who do not have dominion over their sensitivities.

My hope is that after reading this guide you will have the knowledge you need to move forward in life with confidence.

How Will This Book Help?

The Highly Sensitive Person's Growth Guide is intended to provide you with a road map for controlling your sensitivities and presenting yourself more assertively to the world.

With the strategies discussed, you will finally learn to use your HSP strengths in a way that aligns with your purpose. You will finally be able to embrace the real you once you fully understand and manage your high sensitivity traits.

How Is This Book Structured?

This book is divided into nine chapters. In the first chapter, I will define high sensitivity and discuss its common symptoms. I will also talk about the consequences of childhood neglect as it relates to being a highly sensitive adult. You will then be given a brief self-assessment quiz to determine whether you are indeed a highly sensitive person.

In the second chapter, we'll go over specific techniques for mastering emotional regulation. You will learn how to recognize and manage overwhelming feelings as well as handle negative emotions as they arise. You will also learn how to cope with overstimulation, where you will be provided with the most effective techniques to overcome your reaction to highly stimulating environments.

The third chapter addresses the all-too-common issue of guilt and shame frequently experienced by HSPs. You will learn how to overpower your tendency to experience this emotion and identify when it is a false response.

Chapter four dives heavily into the techniques of effective communication skills for the highly sensitive. We'll talk about how to embrace your point of view, manage your anxieties, and be more assertive with others. After reading this chapter, you'll be well on your way to improving your overall interpersonal dynamics.

In chapter five, we'll talk about how to be successful in the workplace as a highly sensitive person. You will learn how to deal with common workplace issues such as overanalyzing and working in a stimulating environment. You will also learn how to make the most of your strengths and avoid becoming stagnant in your career.

Chapter six delves into the more personal side of things, offering strategies for dealing with common relationship issues and partner dissatisfaction.

You will learn how to identify and balance common HSP characteristics in a relationship in order to avoid conflict.

In chapter seven, you will learn how to set boundaries, which is an important life skill. This section will teach you about the power of saying "no," and how limiting yourself in a loving way can lead to deeper connections and the ability to fully express your unique talents and abilities.

In chapter eight, you will learn how to optimize your home organization to be best suited for an HSP. You will discover the minimalist secrets to maximizing your space to soothe your sensitivities.

Last but not least, in chapter nine, you will be provided with parting advice on how to continue to refine your abilities and improve your life as a highly sensitive person. You will learn strategies for increasing your self-esteem and developing your unique abilities.

Now that you understand the fundamentals of this book and how it will benefit you in the long run, let's get started. What you are about to learn may appear difficult at first, but it will be well worth your time. In the next chapter, you will take the first step toward understanding common high sensitivity symptoms, as well as, how your upbringing influences your ability to function as a highly sensitive adult.

Ready? Let's begin!

Chapter 1. Living With High Sensitivity

If you are reading this book, you may have been told that you are too sensitive or that you overthink. You may have been told to tolerate excessive environmental noise. The world around you even suggests that being a very sensitive person is a bad thing. You might feel compelled to rectify or overcome a character "defect" just to be accepted by others. The truth is, people who are highly sensitive are more creative, empathic, sympathetic, and understanding than the rest of the general population. All of these traits need to be celebrated.

With that being said, highly sensitive people do become easily unsettled, overwhelmed and resistant to change. These factors can be difficult to manage and have a negative impact on one's life. However, you can best deal with them by absorbing the unique aspects of your personality and find ways to capitalize on your traits while working around their limitations.

What is High Sensitivity, Exactly?

A highly sensitive person is an individual who deeply processes and has an acute response to both internal and external stimuli. It is a personality trait known as sensory processing sensitivity where the central nervous system is highly attuned to physical, mental and social stimuli.

As a result, HSPs are more physically and emotionally sensitive than others. High sensitivity is generally seen as a normal and healthy personality feature; but as with all personality qualities, it has advantages and disadvantages that must be considered.

Ultimately, HSPs have a stronger emotional response to experiences than the normal individual. They are more sensitive to external information, which makes it more difficult for them to cope with loud noises, large crowds, and stressful situations. Popular author Dr. Elaine Aron attributes high sensitivity to 15 to 20% of the population.

HSPs are born with a biological difference that results in a greater awareness of subtleties and information processing. They are more creative and insightful than others, but they are also more prone to stress and feeling overwhelmed. A highly sensitive person will most likely be consumed with empathy, emotion, and accurately reading social situations. Thus, HSPs are acutely aware of their surroundings.

Highly sensitive people prefer a more leisurely pace and take their time absorbing subtle experiences. Rather than being pleased by a loud concert or a crowded event, an HSP may be more pleased by the smell of their morning coffee and the view from their window. This makes sense for those who are prone to overstimulation: small pleasures and a lighter schedule allow them to do their best without feeling overwhelmed.

It's important to note that although sensitivity is frequently regarded as a personality trait, it is still not officially recognized as one of the American Psychological Association's Big Five personality traits.

Common Signs of a Highly Sensitive Person

Each HSP has a unique experience that is based on their present stage in life. The following are the most typical and pronounced symptoms that a highly sensitive person can experience. See if you are able to identify with any of the following:

- **You are terrified of change.**

    HSPs are at ease in their routines because they are less stimulating than new ones. That is why change, both good and bad, has the potential to destroy HSPs. For example, when you meet someone new or get a job promotion, HSPs may experience an elevated level of stress. HSPs typically require more time to adjust to change than other types of people.

- **You have been misunderstood.**

  The term "high sensitivity" involves being frequently misunderstood. Perhaps you were labeled as "shy" or "anxious," even though you were not truly feeling that way.

- **You're unable to handle criticism**

  Words are extremely important to HSPs. Positive words can send them skyrocketing, but harsh words can send them plummeting. Criticism can be as sharp as a dagger, and the negative consequences can be toxic to a highly sensitive person.

- **Time constraints cause you stress.**

  Timed tests in school made you extremely anxious, possibly to the point of being unable to function normally. As an adult, you become very overwhelmed when you have too many tasks on your to-do list and very little time to complete. Time pressure is not your friend.

- **You're frequently jittery.**

  You jump like a scared cat when someone sneaks up behind you. Many HSPs have a strong "startle reflex," which occurs when their nervous systems are activated even in nonthreatening situations.

- **You tend to withdraw most of the time.**

  Regardless of whether you are an introvert or an extrovert, you require a significant amount of downtime, preferably in solitude. After a long day, you often retreat to a quiet, darkened room to reduce your level of stimulation, ease your senses and recharge.

- **You despise all forms of cruelty and violence.**

  Everyone despises violence and cruelty, but seeing or hearing it can be particularly distressing for those who are overly sensitive. If you find it difficult to watch extremely terrifying or violent movies without becoming distraught or ill, you may be an HSP. Similarly, you will not tolerate a news story about animal cruelty or other horrific acts.

- **You are exhausted from absorbing other people's emotions.**

  Highly sensitive people have a tendency to "soak up" other people's emotions. It is not uncommon for an HSP to walk into a room and instantly feel the mood of the people in it. This is due to the fact that people with high sensitivities are acutely aware of subtleties such as facial expressions, linguistics, and voice tone that others may overlook. When combined with the sensitive person's inherent capacity for empathy, HSPs are not phased that their feelings are not their own. As a result, individuals with a high level of sensitivity commonly encounter emotional stress.

- **You have a problem with conflict.**

  You are intensely aware of any friction or conflict in your close relationships. Numerous HSPs describe experiencing bodily discomfort during times of argument. As a result, some highly sensitive people avoid conflict and will do or say anything to please the other person because it causes so much internal distress.

- **You are flustered by loud noises.**

  A loud motorcycle, fire engine or helicopter roaring through your window can really shake up an HSP.

- **You have a lower tolerance for physical pain.**

  Many types of pain, such as headaches, bodily aches, and wounds, are more painful to HSPs than they are to non-HSPs.

Despite the negative symptoms just mentioned, HSPs can also experience symptoms with positive characteristics. Here are the most common:

- **You are deeply moved by beauty.**

  Fine dining, rich fragrances, lovely artwork, and stirring melodies all have a profound effect on you. The way the wind catches the leaves in the fall sunlight may transport you to a state of near-trance, or you may be transfixed by certain pieces of music or sounds. You simply cannot understand why beauty does not move other people as much as it does you.

- **Your clothing is very important.**

  You are always conscious of what you are wearing. Restrictive clothing might irritate you. Non-HSPs may dislike the same thing, but an HSP carefully selects their wardrobe to avoid it entirely.

- **You have an excessive amount of curiosity.**

  HSPs are constantly on the lookout for answers to life's most pressing concerns. These individuals are baffled as to why things have turned out the way they have and what their own function is in this whole situation. It is possible that you have always pondered why the secrets of human nature and the world do not intrigue others in the same way.

- **You think deeply.**

  Your profound internal processing is the foundation of HSP. This means you have a lot more to think about regarding your experiences. Unfortunately, this also increases your proclivity to overthink in a negative manner. You may find yourself excessively replaying events in your head or spiraling into worrisome thoughts.

The Impact of Childhood Neglect

If you consider yourself to be highly sensitive, you must understand that your childhood experiences will have a disproportionately large impact on your well-being as an adult. Although the effects of a difficult childhood may impact you more than others, that doesn't mean you can't or shouldn't try to address those effects.

Even though high sensitivity is referred to as a "nature" trait rather than a "nurture" trait, your upbringing will have an impact on your overall well-being. Sensitivity does not "improve" or "decrease"; rather, it is determined by how you interact with it. For example, if you were well-adjusted as a child because your high sensitivity was valued and rewarded, you are more likely to remain so as an adult.

However, if you were embarrassed as a child due to your sensitivity, you may be unaware of the appropriate methods to help you manage your sensitivity as an adult. You might find that when you focus on this "flaw", you may begin to dislike yourself.

What happens when the trait is not emphasized or valued?

Studies have revealed that many relatively stable families fail to recognize or respond to the emotional needs of their children, resulting in their being raised in emotional neglect. This can be harmful to any child, but sensitive children are especially vulnerable. When one's emotional needs go unmet, one feels unappreciated and empty.

The most common cause of childhood neglect is a parent's failure to meet the child's emotional needs when they arise. This neglect may appear minor at first, but to a child, it has the same effect as emotional or physical abuse and can lead to profound loneliness. Because of this, HSPs grow up with unresolved feelings of shame, regret or low self-esteem.

These findings are due to the fact that HSPs use emotions as their first language. A family that ignores their child's emotional needs is not speaking this language. While parents clearly experience emotions, they attempt to suppress or conceal their own as well as those of others. Simply put, they are isolating themselves from their HSP child's most important inner self. Children who have experienced emotional neglect learn that asking for help can lead to rejection or being labeled as "weak." HSP children must then learn to advocate for their own needs in a world that frequently does not understand them.

It should come as no surprise that a child with low self-esteem comes to distrust and devalue themselves. When neglectful parents are unable to recognize or validate their child's strengths and feelings, they may view their child's shyness as a deficiency and attempt to force their child to feel more secure.

HSPs in general have a difficult time dealing with criticism, which is almost always stressful for a child. Children with high-functioning autism (HFA) do not receive effective feedback if they have experienced emotional neglect. Furthermore, it is unrealistic to expect children to learn appropriate coping strategies if they have never witnessed them demonstrated at home.

When a child is highly sensitive, their parents can only accommodate their needs if they are sympathetic. If not, they believe the child is exaggerating and may become irritated with them. When a child is overwhelmed, he or she may experience increased anxiety.

Consequently, emotional neglect in childhood does not go away as you get older. As adults carry it into their lives, it affects everything an HSP touches, whether it's relationships, self-image, or mental well-being. HSPs who are recovering from neglect keep their emotions buried, or they may become "numb" as a result of the walled-off nature of their emotions. Only when they are overwhelmed do highly sensitive people express their desires (or withdraw completely).

Fortunately, emotional neglect experienced during childhood can be remedied. As an adult HSP, you should be able to express your emotions during routine, day-to-day conversations. You will notice that when you begin to treat yourself with respect and dignity, the people in your life will begin to recognize and respond to you in a different way. After they get to know you, they begin to understand your personality, feelings, and needs.

More importantly, they begin to focus on the real you.

Self Assessment Quiz

At this point, you may still be unsure about your HSP status after reading over the many symptoms and characteristics of this trait. The following is a short quiz that will quickly assist in determining your status.

Answer each statement based on how you personally feel. Answer 'yes' if it is somewhat true for you; answer 'no' if it is not very true or not true at all for you.

1. Being extremely hungry causes a strong reaction in me, which interferes with my ability to concentrate and maintain a positive attitude.

   Yes ____ No ____

2. My nerves get a little jittery when there is change in my personal life.

   Yes ____ No ____

3. It is very easy for me to become overwhelmed by disconcerting stimuli such as flashing lights, strong odors, coarse fabrics, or sirens.

   Yes ____ No ____

4. I consider myself to be a person of high moral character.

   Yes ____ No ____

5. I have a proclivity to be startled at any given moment.

   Yes ____ No ____

6. Being forced to do too many things at the same time makes me irritable.

   Yes ____ No ____

7. Beautiful artwork, smells, sounds, and tastes spark my interest and deepen my appreciation for them.

   Yes ____ No ____

8. I place a high value on planning my life in order to avoid being confronted with stressful or overwhelming circumstances.

   Yes ____ No ____

9. Extreme stimuli, such as loud noises or chaotic scenes, make me feel uncomfortable.

   Yes ___ No ___

10. The moods of others have an impact on my own feelings and thoughts.

    Yes ___ No ___

11. I'm someone who is extremely sensitive to physical discomfort or pain.

    Yes ___ No ___

12. In times of stress, I need to go to my bed, a darker room, or somewhere else where I may have some privacy and rest from stimulation when my day is very chaotic.

    Yes ___ No ___

If you answered 'yes' to six or more of these statements, then you are most likely a highly sensitive person.

It is common for you to feel misunderstood by others due to your sensitivity. Every HSP must occasionally deal with bouts of overstimulation or overwhelm. HSPs are also more sensitive to their surroundings, whether they are supportive or harmful. As a result, being highly sensitive can appear to be both a blessing and a curse at times in one's life. You should be aware, however, that testing as a highly sensitive person is not only natural and good, but it is also a powerful skill set for many people.

Chapter 2. Mastering Emotional Regulation

Highly sensitive people tend to think carefully about everything since their strong emotions such as curiosity, anxiety, joy, or anger encourage them to do so. However, this intensity can be overwhelming, especially if you are experiencing negativity. For this reason, it is important to learn proper emotional regulation skills.

What is emotional regulation and how does it work?

Emotional regulation is defined as an action that we all do intuitively or unconsciously to influence our mood. For instance, if you find yourself feeling angry, you might take a stroll through the park. If you find something funny, but it's not appropriate to laugh, you might keep your chuckle to yourself. These types of responses are examples of emotional regulation in play.

It should be noted that the basic definition of emotional regulation states that this behavior is unconscious and our actions were most likely taught to us as children or adopted during a stressful situation. However, not everyone is taught how to respond to adversity by regulating their emotions at a young age. For many HSPs, developing a sense of emotional regulation in adulthood can be difficult due to the lack of self-regulation skills acquired during childhood.

Negative emotions can strike harder in those with high sensitivity because they are built to see the environment with increased emotional "clarity."
Because the parts of an HSP's brain that process emotions are literally more active than those of non-HSPs, the highly sensitive person may experience an erratic fluctuation of emotion. A rollercoaster ride of feelings can accompany an HSP when they are dealing with any kind of life change. You can be overjoyed one minute, and then panicked and tortured by the prospect of dealing with it the next-- even if it's something positive like receiving a promotion at work.

While dealing with happy emotions can be an exciting experience, it can be completely overwhelming when dealing with negative ones. For example, a single source of anxiety can cause you to become unable to function for several days, such as being concerned that a friend or coworker is secretly enraged at you.

Due to these extreme sentiments, many highly sensitive people believe they have a problem or wish they could get rid of their sensitivity permanently. HSPs deal with "more" emotions because they tend to take in other people's feelings (or the vibe of an entire room). They not only have to deal with their own negative feelings, but also those of everyone else.

Imagine the following scenario: your spouse is stressed out as a result of an incident that occurred at work. They return home crabby and spend the rest of the evening sulking around the house. Soon after, despite the fact that you had a good day, you begin to feel stressed as well simply as a result of the energy he or she is emitting.

That tendency of the HSP to easily take on the emotional states of others is a continual source of conflict. When you're feeling things so deeply and picking up on them everywhere you go, it's necessary to take some time to figure out what you're feeling and why you're feeling it. Are you feeling nervous about the outcome of your job interview? Is it because the interviewer appeared to be distracted, or is it something else? What about that supposedly "rude" encounter on the way to the interview? Maybe the coffee shop barista was having a bad day and didn't realize that his body language was exclaiming it.

Sure, most people experience this inner conflict to some degree, but for highly sensitive people, absorbing others' emotions is a very real struggle that they face on a daily basis. They can find themselves harboring anger, sadness, or anxiety that aren't even their fault. Other times, they are unquestionably their own but they are experiencing them with such intensity that it is difficult to imagine overcoming it. However, if you understand how to harness the power of your sensitivity, emotional regulation as an HSP does not have to be as difficult as it first seems. To get "unstuck," you need to take a step back and begin processing your thoughts and feelings in a way that is helpful. You need to develop a healthy set of self regulation skills.

Understanding and Managing Your Negative Emotions

If you're an anxious, highly sensitive person, you know how critical it is to learn healthy ways to manage your emotions. Here are the most effective methods for processing and moving past negative feelings:

1. Observe and live with your emotions for a brief period.

Highly sensitive people seem to have difficulty with the notion that their emotions are incorrect. In some ways, the emotion reflects a failure to deliver on one's expectations. As a result, they attempt to suppress them.

To remedy this, the best course of action is to simply accept the emotion as a normal part of the human spectrum. If you are angry, don't you wish you could be feeling something other than irritation? Of course you do. However, it is also acceptable that you are agitated in the moment and pushing it away will only prolong the duration of the entire situation. What you oppose will continue to exist.

When you are feeling anxious or hurt, you want to move that negative feeling as far away as possible without hurting yourself. There is a caveat, though, in that you must first feel those emotions in order to be able to totally release them.

This could be as simple as sitting quietly somewhere safe (like being wrapped in a warm blanket) and working through the issues at hand. Some helpful strategies for genuinely unblocking and processing an emotion include journaling, confiding with a trusted friend, and, in some cases, crying out loud. Crying itself can be nature's way of expressing how one is truly feeling. It also detoxifies the body and can even help to dull pain. Depending on whether you're in a safe environment, you might even yell, punch a pillow, or tear up paper. All of these things help to move the feeling forward and get you out of a rut.

2. Do not be ashamed of the feelings that arise when they do.

This is something with which I have found many HSPs to have a lot of difficulty. A portion of this can be traced back to the higher rates of perfectionism found in highly sensitive people. If they are experiencing an unpleasant emotion, it is a sign that they have flaws. Being flawed also implies that one is not deserving of affection. In order to respond more effectively, you should treat yourself in the same way that you would a good friend. Do you believe that your loved ones become less lovable when they are suffering? Most likely not. The same can be applied to conversations with yourself. It is important to accept the emotions that arise from whatever situation they stemmed. Feeling ashamed will not allow you to progress in regulating them. Acceptance in the moment is a must.

3. Stay away from emotional triggers that are negative.

Do you know what doesn't help when dealing with negativity? More doom and gloom. It doesn't matter where it originates or how well-intentioned the individual is who sent it. Any form of negative influence stifles recovery when dealing with adverse feelings. When dealing with unpleasant emotions, you must avoid any form of stress factors in order to prevent more damage to your emotional health.

Avoid watching the news because it is nearly always negative. Move your attention away from those who seem to be on the lookout for anything to complain about or who are solely preoccupied with negativity. Observe your relationships with the people in your life and reflect on your feelings after spending time with them. If you always find yourself feeling worse after meeting with a specific person, then it's time to make some adjustments - can you reduce time spent with them or avoid seeing them altogether? If there are some individuals who are unavoidable, such as a coworker or your mother-in-law, then it is time to develop appropriate boundaries for yourself, which will be discussed in a later chapter.

4. Take care of your body as much as your mind.

HSPs are more likely to experience negative emotions when they are tired, haven't eaten properly, or become stressed. Emotions can appear to be all-consuming, but they are actually a part of your body. Even though it is only a "feeling," it causes physical reactions in you, such as an increase in cortisol (the stress hormone) or an increase in heart rate. Taking care of your physical well-being is an important part of dealing with these negative feelings.

As simple as it may seem, eating regularly and consuming plenty of nutritious foods, exercising, and getting enough sleep all contribute to good health and wellness. These are fundamental, and chances are that one of them will serve as a more important foundation for you than the others. Increased physical activity can help you lose weight while also increasing your endorphin levels and protecting your body from the dangerous effects of stress. The ability to "clear out" negative emotions and process one's experiences is critical for highly sensitive people — who may require a little more sleep than the average person.

5. Accept that emotions are temporary.

When these intense feelings strike, they can feel so overwhelming that they seem far beyond your control. Moreover, when you look around, you may not see anyone else who appears to be paralyzed by a bad mood. This only serves to exacerbate the situation. If they aren't buckling under the pressure, it must be because you are simply less capable than they are. However, this is not the case. Everyone is dealing with their own set of difficulties. And the majority of people are concealing their difficulties and vulnerabilities in the same way that you might be.

Remember negative emotions are only temporary. When you start to feel yourself slipping into a particularly dark place, you have the distinct impression that the sensation will last for an eternity. This, of course, doesn't make any sense on an intellectual level, but emotionally you feel as if it will never come to an end.

In the event that you are dissatisfied with your significant other, a shadow can fall over your entire perspective of the relationship. Is it possible that things will continue in this manner? You think that maybe you should get out now before it's too late and you both end up miserable for the rest of your lives. But then the feeling goes away. The intensity begins to wane. You make up and life goes on as usual. It's critical to remember that these feelings are normal, even though they are most likely only temporary in nature.

6. Avoid "black and white" thinking.

We commonly get stuck in negative emotions because they feel big and overwhelming at the time. It's as if we have to face the world alone or our problem will overtake us no matter how hard we try to stop it. This is known as "black and white thinking," or the inclination to think in extremes. You're either a dazzling success or a total disaster. It's a mental stumbling block that can amplify bad feelings. When you use terms like "always" or "never," you may discover yourself getting into an all-or-nothing mindset. Often, the truth lies somewhere in the middle.

When you are faced with only two options, remind yourself that there are always alternatives, as well as multiple solutions to your problem. Make a list of those alternatives, beginning with the first three options on the list. Furthermore, keep in mind that you will never be able to anticipate exactly what will happen in any given circumstance, so let go of that responsibility right now. Then consider, "What do I have control over?" What can I do to assist? This is usually the point where you stop feeling helpless and start seeing a way forward.

7. Make a deliberate effort to reconnect with your body to step out of your head.

When you're anxious, try speeding up your breathing and heart rate to match your racing thoughts. When your heart and mind are racing, it is often preferable to first accelerate rather than try to force everything to slow down. Take a quick stroll around the block. You could also go for a jog if or do push-ups if you prefer. Anything that gets your body moving will do.

Movement aids in the burning off of the adrenaline that has been coursing through your body. You can then begin to gradually slow the process back down once your body has caught up with your mental state of mind. Are you unable to do strenuous movements? Make use of power poses. The way you sit can also have an impact on your mental state and physiological well-being.

That being said, you can also use physical sensation to help you relax and bring yourself back to normal. Among the relaxation triggers are deep breathing exercises, yoga or calm tea like chamomile. Hot showers are also effective because they are not only relaxing, but cleansing as well. You can even use visualization to your advantage. While taking a shower, visualize yourself scrubbing away negativity and inviting in more positive energy.

Consider the physical sensations or rituals that help you to feel calmer, more centered, and less stressed. Your body will learn to identify the physical cue with the healing process as soon as you employ the habits anytime you're feeling overwhelmed by a bad emotion. As a result, your overall health will improve dramatically.

8. Find a way to express yourself creatively.

We all require some form of creative expression. And there's something for everyone, whether you like to write, paint, sing, or do needlework. The best way for highly sensitive people to cope with difficult emotional states is to have a channel through which they can move through the emotion. Being extremely sensitive to your surroundings, putting that intensity to good use in the form of something constructive is the best way to redirect it. It should come as no surprise that incredible works of art have emerged from tragic events or bad experiences.

9. Make your surroundings supportive of your body's natural rhythms.

HSPs perform best when they have regular places to recharge. They also thrive on a set schedule. Make your bedroom a relaxing haven where you can unwind at the end of the day. As a result of this, rest and sleep will be improved. To avoid seasonal affective disorder (also known as SAD), turn on a full spectrum light in the early morning hours during the winter. Make an effort to keep your workplace tidy and attractive. Keep lavender essential oils on hand to help you feel more at ease when faced with a difficult situation. Carry a set of earphones with you so that you can listen to soothing music or follow a guided meditation session. Be proactive and do everything you can to ensure that your environment is supportive of you.

10. Maintain a healthy blood sugar level.

If you're getting foggy-headed and irritable, it's time to check your hunger levels. As a general rule of thumb, avoid having difficult conversations with other people if you are hungry. It will have no positive outcome. This shouldn't be too challenging unless the conversation is about "where should we eat?"

With this in mind, it's also a good idea to cut back on stimulants. Caffeine and sugar are strongly disliked by many HSPs, owing to their increased sensitivity. Begin paying attention to your body's reactions to these chemicals and eliminate anything that interferes.

11. Develop a mindfulness-based practice that you can stick to.

This could be a form of meditation or yoga. Essentially, you want to create a practice that will assist you in developing the ability to observe your thoughts from a distance. When your emotions are triggered, you're essentially being taken over by them. There is a feeling of being swept downstream by the current of your mind, as if it were a fast-moving river. It's like getting out of the river and standing on a bank to observe the current of your thoughts.

The parasympathetic nervous system, which aids in sleep and digestion, is activated when we practice mindful breathing. The simplest approach is to inhale through the nose and exhale through pursed lips to create a little bubble. Diaphragmatic and square breathing can also be beneficial.

Instead of suppressing your nervous system during stressful situations, practice grounding, which allows your nervous system to return to normal and helps you relax. You can ground yourself by focusing on your breathing or simply meditating on the sensations of the earth beneath your feet, taking in the colors and textures of your surroundings, practicing mild yoga, bathing in a hot tub, or using a weighted blanket.

Highly sensitive people have a proclivity to experience negative emotions with a particular level of intensity. As self-aware as you are, this is an unfortunate side effect. When the emotion takes hold, HSPs often report having the impression that the feeling will last forever. Those low points have become a part of you. They are every bit as important and valuable as the highs, if not more so. They are, of course, unpleasant, and the danger is that if you do not learn to cope with them, you may find yourself trapped by them.

Keep in mind that negative emotions are there to help you feel balanced, to teach you a lesson, and to help you be grateful for the good times in your life. However, this does not imply that you must remain in them indefinitely.

Encourage yourself to believe in your ability to influence your environment, change the situation, and overcome the difficulties you may be facing. When life is spinning out of control, do not believe that you are powerless to stop it. Ultimately, we all have the ability to make a difference in our own lives. Even though we have no control over our emotions or the circumstances that contributed to their development, we do, however, have the ability to influence them.

How To Cope With Overstimulation

When we are infants, we learn to regulate our emotions through our interactions with our parents. As adults, these abilities are utilized on a regular basis without our thinking. As previously mentioned, the term "emotional regulation" refers to the ability to adjust and regulate one's own feelings, particularly when they are severe and unpleasant. Although we should not stop feeling altogether or simply "feel nice", we should learn to tolerate our sensations and emotional arousal more effectively so that we do not feel powerless in the face of them. Long-term psychological issues can arise as a result of a deficiency in this area.

If you're a highly sensitive adult, chances are you were a highly sensitive child. It's very likely that, when you wept as a child, your parents tried to comfort and soothe you because of your restlessness. It's also possible they may have held you close, whispering softly or humming to provide a comforting distraction. This made you feel better by helping you relax and release stress in your body and mind. The truth is, that by consciously applying similar techniques, we can continue strengthening and developing our ability to control and regulate emotions in adulthood.

When you're experiencing emotional overstimulation, the best thing you can do is regulate your emotions. When you were a child, you would not have stopped sobbing if your parents had yelled at you, reprimanded you, or shut you in a room by yourself. Because of this, you must be able to control your emotions in challenging situations rather than condemning your inclination to become too agitated. This only serves to increase the amount of tension you feel and increase your level of irritation, rather than aiding in your ability to calm down more quickly.

There is no doubt that being overcome with emotion or overstimulated to the point where you feel the need to flee is an upsetting experience, but there are ways to reduce your stress and regain control quickly. If you find yourself experiencing overstimulation, here are some tried-and-true methods to help recover:

Seek silence.

Find a quiet place that you enjoy, such as your room, the library, a bookshop, or a museum. Cafes are wonderful, but they can be very noisy, so if everything is too loud for you, go to a place where you are confident that silence is respected and appreciated. It's important to remember that the closest quiet space may not always be in your own home; however, an isolated public park or lake is almost always a safe bet.

Engage in familiar music.

Play a song from your own playlist that you are familiar with and feel close to. For those who are easily distressed, new sensory input might be upsetting, yet familiar sounds can be soothing on occasion.

Put your phone on airplane mode or turn it off.

Leaving your phone in another, or going for a long walk without using it, are all excellent alternatives. When utilizing this strategy, it might be extremely beneficial to keep yourself away from distracting stimuli like television and radio.

Focus on the present by closing your eyes.

As a matter of instinct, people who are experiencing sensory overload will close their eyes and cover their ears to protect themselves. In some circumstances, taking these precautions may help you avoid any extreme reactions. Surprisingly, the simple act of closing your eyes can sometimes assist you in dealing with excessive noise. The brain is not aware of the distinction and is only aware of the fact that it has a large amount of sensory data to process.

Indulge yourself with artistic creations.

Look for something beautiful and allow yourself to be absorbed by it. Literature, artwork, music, street art, or anything else could be included in this category. Allow yourself to be moved by what you are seeing. The amount of energy that can be gained is tremendous.

Politely request silence from others.

Many HSPs skip this tactic given their desire to avoid becoming a nuisance to others. While it isn't appropriate for use in every environment, like a construction site, you can tell your coworkers or roommate what you require if someone won't stop talking or is listening to loud music.

It's appropriate to say, "I've been going through a pretty tough period and I'm feeling overstimulated. Are you okay with staying quiet for a little while?"

If possible, leave the situation.

Pay attention to your inner feelings and get out of any circumstance that makes you feel stressed out. If you're within an office building, the ideal solution is to go outside; but, if you're in a noisy or packed room, simply leaving the room itself will do. If you are outside and its busy, locate a quiet space to sit. It's easy to find solitude and silence in single stall bathrooms or a car when you're pressed for time.

Use the box breathing method to your advantage.

Deep breathing exercises are your best bet if you can't get away from the stressful environment you're in. You can use box breathing when you're feeling stressed or anxious because it is so simple to remember.

When you count to four, take a slow and steady inhale through your nose and hold it. When you count to four again, take a slow and steady exhale through your mouth. Repeat this pattern for a total of four minutes.

Train yourself to use the box breathing technique when you're calm so that you can more easily access it when you're in a frenetic state of mind.

Get some fresh air by going outside.

There's something very calming about taking a stroll through the park or a short hike up your favorite route. It may be immensely peaceful and revitalizing to reconnect with nature when the clamor of daily life becomes too much to bear. In addition, numerous studies have shown that exposure to sunlight improves mood and energy levels. A brisk walk through a quiet neighborhood or office park can also do the trick.

Spend some time reading.

A little bit of healthy escapism is good for the soul, and there's nothing quite like a good book to help you bounce into another world. Furthermore, books are a fantastic way to unwind and unwind well. The University of Sussex found that subjects who read for only six minutes had lower heart rates, less muscle tension, and lower levels of stress than those who did not read at all.

Relieve yourself of the stressful circumstance that has you feeling overburdened by going to your quiet spot and reading something relaxing. To maximize your relaxation, curl up under your favorite blanket with a cup of tea, coffee, or hot cocoa.

Pay attention to your physical appearance.

When we talk about self-care, we frequently refer to engaging in activities that we find particularly soothing or revitalizing, such as cooking, exercising, or engaging in a recreational activity. However, one of the most effective forms of self-care is to actually take care of your body. Pay attention to your body by giving yourself a manicure, following your favorite skin care routine, applying makeup, or shaving with a hot towel to rejuvenate your senses.

Take a long, hot bath.

If you're feeling stressed out, taking a hot bath or shower can help you de-stress more quickly and effectively. When we bathe in warm water, serotonin is released in our brains, which helps to relieve stress. Serotonin, a neurotransmitter, is responsible for the regulation of mood, hunger, sleep, and social functioning. Baths are a wonderful way to unwind while also indulging in some aromatherapy benefits. By combining lavender, rose, or chamomile essential oils with other relaxing ingredients, you can attain even greater relaxation.

Refrain from using social media.

When you're feeling overwhelmed and overstimulated, it's critical to avoid engaging in activities that will aggravate your symptoms even further. Although we all enjoy social media sites, they have unfortunately become increasingly irritating over time (despite our best efforts). As a result of our deep disagreements on so many issues, we're turning to social media to express ourselves.

A large percentage of social media users like and support political and social content, so no matter where you stand on the political or social spectrum, you're bound to see something that enrages or saddens you. Since these kinds of things just serve to increase your sense of despair, avoid using social media if you're feeling unwell.

Shallow vs. deep breathing

In spite of its simplicity, breathing is nevertheless a vital part of being more present and relaxed. When we pay attention to our breathing, we become more centered and engaged in the present moment. Because many people only breathe in and out through their nose and mouth, they are more likely to breathe shallowly than they should be. Deep breathing causes the activation of abdominal muscles, which is why it is commonly referred to as "belly breathing". Taking quick breaths is a natural response to feelings of dread, worry, or when in "survival mode." Deep breathing sends a signal to our brains that everything is fine, allowing us to relax our bodies and minds at the same time.

Close your eyes or lower your gaze to see if you're taking deep breaths or skipping them altogether. To find out if you're breathing deeply or shallowly, place your hands on your stomach and your chest. Inhale and exhale slowly. Your breathing will be shallower and faster if all you move is your chest.

You can practice belly breathing by inhaling deeply through your nose. Try to imagine air going from your nose, down your neck, past your lungs, and into the lower part of your abdomen as you breathe in and out via your mouth. Be patient if your chest feels tight or constrained when you first try this. Inhale deeply and slowly through your nose before doing this. Exhale for as long as it takes to get all the air out of your lungs and stomach. The exhale is crucial if you're trying to relax using your breath.

Swallowing triggers the sympathetic nervous system, the region of the brain that controls our fight-or-flight reaction. A component of our neural system that is engaged only while the body is at rest gets activated when we exhale. Take a deep breath in and exhale a sigh of relief when you're taken completely by surprise. Extending your exhale engages the same part of your nervous system as did the prior approach of communicating your state of relaxation to your brain and body.

A person's predisposition to become overstimulated cannot be completely avoided because there is no stressful situation in life that can be fully avoided —whether it's an outing to the grocery store, a friend's birthday party, giving a presentation at work or booking your next vacation. Each one of these scenarios has the potential to become overstimulating due to the processing of various stimuli. As a result, it is not possible to avoid exposure, because doing so would result in a life that is extremely controlled and boring.

It is sometimes necessary to accept brief periods of overstimulation in order to maintain an active lifestyle, take risks, pursue life goals, and learn new things. Moreover, even though overstimulation is unpleasant, it is only harmful to your health if you continue to be in a chronic state of exposure for an extended period of time without giving your nervous system a break. Therefore, highly sensitive people should practice calming themselves down in order to become less sensitive in the future.

Chapter 3. Controlling Guilt and Shame as an HSP

Have you ever felt bad because you couldn't help someone in need or had to decline someone's request? Driving a family member to the airport in the middle of the night after working late and being pressured to socialize with coworkers is the definition of a stressful situation. As a result of guilt and obligation, you may have said "yes" even when your internal voice screamed "no."

The challenges of living as an HSP might make it difficult to take care of oneself and set healthy boundaries, such as having to meet social norms and being uneasy with conflict. Dealing with the stress and guilt that comes from caring for oneself is one of the most difficult challenges for the highly sensitive person. You would rather disappoint others than hurt their feelings, so you sacrifice your own desires to help them.

For the highly sensitive, the guilt intensity dial appears to be higher than that of the other 80% of the population. HSPs become much more distressed when someone else is upset. They will try to help even if their own tank is completely empty and have nothing to offer, because it may save someone else's life or serve as an alternative to feeling guilty. Highly sensitive people have a tendency to please others, which results in a greater sense of ease when obliging a request, as opposed to managing the sensations of another's distress or confronting the frustrations of their energetic limitations.

The sensation of guilt is multifaceted, and it can elicit a variety of emotions such as worry, regret, grief and self-doubt. HSPs understandably want to avoid unpleasant feelings of guilt for as long as possible, but this will only help in the short term. Long-term consequences of these sacrifices include resentment, anger, anxiety, and sadness.

Shame and guilt are all socially acceptable emotions. You can't have it if you don't have others nearby. Shame appears to exist to keep us in the good graces of our social group, punishing us for any minor transgression. Because we, as humans, used to live in groups, our very survival was dependent on them. We'd be kicked out of the group if we kept behaving badly.

When you believe you have done something wrong, your guilt is less severe than when you believe you are not evil. Even if you are not truly guilty, the guilt itself has no finality.

Is Guilt Always Real?

Guilt is widely regarded as a debt, and frequently assumed by most people that it can be repaid through suffering. We believe that if we just keep completing certain actions, the guilt will go away.

Emotions, on the other hand, do not work in this manner. If you don't process them properly, they'll just sit in your digestive tract like a massive, fatty rock. Having said that, it is a mistake to believe that the feeling of guilt is always warranted. There are some truly toxic people in the world, with a strange but incredibly persuasive gift that allows them to make others feel guilty for things that are, by any measure, absolutely necessary to human survival. Do you know any of those people? They appear to sow seeds of guilt with every word they speak.

Do some research before succumbing to your own feelings of guilt. How many of those people have you had contact with, and how long have you had contact with them? Is it possible that they bear a large portion of the blame? It's pointless to try to pay your dues if it doesn't work. There is no debt owed by you.

As strong as that feeling of guilt appears to be, it is a false flag. It appears and acts like guilt, but when examined closely, you will discover that you have no reason to feel sorry. Fake guilt is like fake money; it circulates no matter how hard we try to get rid of it and is still used as currency. However, because it is a forgery, it must be destroyed.

The Origin of HSP Shame

Without a doubt, HSPs have a greater capacity for shame than others. While it is true that they feel emotions more intensely, this is due in part to their increased awareness of them. Because they have heightened sensitivity, they can employ a strategy of being mindful and cautious before acting. The negative feelings associated with shame encourage them to avoid or conceal anything that might cause others to dislike them. Furthermore, they are considerate and do not want to cause harm, and can anticipate the long-term consequences of their actions. Simply put, they are hardwired to recognize shame and to resist impulses that would lead to it.

HSPs are more affected by poor parenting, particularly physical or emotional punishments such as shaming, but they can also experience shame as a result of being ignored, abandoned, or unloved. Even if it doesn't make sense, it motivates them as children to work harder in order to receive the love and care they require.

Most people blame others for things they didn't do or minimize their responsibility by saying things like, "I didn't really mean to do that," or "that wasn't really part of my job." They may also try to give the impression that they are unafraid of what they have done by saying, "This does not relate to me—I am beyond all that," or "I simply don't care what others think of me." In some cases, they make someone else feel inferior: "I cannot believe how upset you are about this." While people with a high sensitivity personality can use all of these coping mechanisms, I believe they use them less because they avoid embarrassing behavior in the first place. They adapt to the preferences of others. Their goal is to be flawless, error-free, and extremely generous. They accomplish more than they believe they can, so no one can say they haven't tried or accomplished anything.

Unfortunately, this attention to detail can sometimes lead to severe limitations in one's life. Because shame does not make us feel horrible, we rarely notice when we are not feeling shame. We are also not being spontaneous, warm, or loving. We're not reaching out our hands to get what we want, nor are we thinking about what made us happy. At the very least, we are not ashamed, until we come to that realization and then feel ashamed that we did nothing about it.

Almost everyone has a childhood memory of being embarrassed, shamed, or humiliated. For some, the mistake was made when they were potty trained, when they were punished by staying in their room, or when they were spanked for something they were not. That realization was especially upsetting for those who realized they differed from the majority in a way that was unacceptable. We felt shame, either because of our sensitivity or because of how others reacted. For example, children who are caught stealing frequently experience feelings of guilt, but children who are particularly sensitive may experience more deeply ingrained shame, especially if the parent reacts harshly.

It is acceptable to consider the moment of shame to be the point at which one officially becomes a member of the human race. Your capacity to experience shame's dreadful anguish has been activated, much like becoming the first person to suffer a painful burn. The pain will drive you to work harder to avoid experiencing it again, just as you would work harder to avoid setting yourself on fire.

Remember that shame is linked to your HSP traits because you are empathic and compassionate, which are two essential qualities for relationships, as well as a beloved friend, partner, parent, and relative. Feeling guilty shows that you are concerned about others and their well-being. That is something to strive for, but healthy boundaries and self-care are also essential, which will be discussed in a separate chapter.

Getting over your fear of shame entails receiving a lot of advice on how to live your life. You must fortify yourself. The most important thing is to genuinely love yourself and exude self-assurance.

Even if we don't completely eliminate guilt, we can work to reduce it and eventually transform it into self-acceptance. It is about listening to our inner voice and being willing to put ourselves first rather than others.

Instead of always doing what someone else wants you to do, consider what you would like to do instead. When you lower your boundaries to care for someone else, it appears that you are foregoing a necessary need. You will avoid anger and estrangement if you act solely in your own self-interest.

When deciding whether or not to respond "yes" to a request, consider your availability to assist at the time. Say "yes" to your friends only on your own terms.

Before you look after someone else, it is important to figure out what your needs are. Detach from perfectionism and duty by practicing self-compassion and turning your empathy inward. Practice saying the following to yourself:

- "I'm doing the best I can with what I've got."
- "Please allow me to be gentle with myself."
- "I want to accept myself exactly as I am"

As an HSP, your capacity to empathize and be kind are two of your highly sensitive strengths. These are the same abilities that make you a great partner, friend, parent, and other member of the family. The fact that you are inclined to feel guilty shows that you have compassion for others and are interested in their well-being. While this isn't necessarily a bad thing, it can be managed with good limits and self-care.

Given our capacity for emotional sensation as well as empathy, we are prone to feeling guilty when not saying "yes" or providing assistance when others ask. Sacrificing our own needs in order to avoid guilt completely may seem like a good idea in the short term, but it will only lead to feelings of resentment, anger, anxiety, and unhappiness in the long run. By prioritizing your own needs and practicing self-compassion, you may transform shame into self-acceptance. As a result, you are free to be your true self and interact with others in a genuine way.

Increasing Self-Esteem

When most people think about their own self-esteem, they are more concerned with the role it plays in their day-to-day activities. When HSPs lack self-confidence, they treat it as if it were a garment that everyone could see and judge them for wearing. If you follow these steps, you'll notice a positive difference in your life.

Accept thoughts, feelings, and sensations for what they are.

Don't pass judgment on them. They are transient in nature and can be altered. They arise within and can be let go of by the mind and body.

Don't rely on others to make you feel valuable.

You will undoubtedly be duped by another person. You must absorb your power and become its sole bearer. No label, position, or affiliation can provide you with value. That is extraneous information. You must ensure that your self-esteem remains intact if something or someone is removed from your life.

Embrace your outside of the box thinking.

HSPs are among the most talented artists on the planet. Why? Because they lean on their curiosity, ask questions about the status quo, and go with the flow when increased sensory processing is combined with a deep interior experience. This distinguishes HSPs from those who are too afraid to dream big and achieve their goals.

Utilize your high level of emotional intelligence.

HSPs have a keen eye for nuance that others may overlook, and can see what is being said without being explicitly told. It may surprise you to learn that highly sensitive people can be excellent professionals and marketers because of their exceptional ability to connect with others, listen, and empathize.

Make it easier to provide feedback to others.

Even if they are good communicators, most sensitive people struggle when they are caught off guard in meetings or presentations. Similarly, a harsh statement may bother them for days or weeks. Prepare yourself for high-stakes conversations if you are an HSP in advance of being questioned. Create a response bank to handle common work questions:

- "Permit me to return to you."

- "That is an excellent question. What are your thoughts on the situation?"
- "Thank you for your input. Allow me some time to process what I just heard."

Don't react. Instead, respond.

In the face of the unexpected, it is essential for you to develop your resilience as a high-functioning personality. Distinguish between your emotional reaction and the triggering event by practicing mindfulness techniques. Avoid allowing anxiety to take control of your life. Stress is more pronounced in high-functioning individuals due to their tendency to experience more intense feelings.

If your partner continues to leave dirty dishes in the sink, it's not a good idea to lash out or, even worse, say nothing at all. Take a deep breath or count to five before reacting in a stressful situation. Doing so allows you to regain control over your impulses.

If you say something you'll later come to regret or realize you didn't mean, ask for a timeout to calm yourself down. Make a list of your thoughts before reacting. It is acceptable to take a break from your relationship before continuing on. It demonstrates your maturity, critical thinking, and good self-control, all of which are qualities in which you should be proud of.

Embrace multiple interests.
You are clearly concerned about your career and relationships. HSPs are smart trailblazers who find ways to combine their diverse interests in successful careers that make a difference in the world.

Be firm with your boundaries.

You must conserve your energy if you are a highly sensitive individual. Every day, you spend your time observing how your colleagues are feeling and how they are behaving. You may feel depleted if these interactions are unfavorable. Noisy, bustling workplaces also irritate HSPs.

Therefore, simple changes can have a significant impact. Try to arrive at the office early in order to enjoy some quiet work before the busy day begins. To ensure that you have time to decompress, schedule 15 to 30 minutes between meetings.

Effective energy management establishes firm boundaries and pays close attention to the inputs you accept in your life. Limit your contact with toxic people, take care of the materials you consume, and look after yourself. If you expect a lot from yourself (as most HSPs do), then planning for rest and recovery intervals is unavoidable.

Assess your abilities.

Everyone on this planet has a gift or a calling. In fact, each of us possesses a wide range of skills that we can use to help others. These must be determined. Start small if you don't know what those skills are. What kind of good deeds are you carrying out? What brings you joy? How do you improve the lives of others? You might be the one in your friend's group who is constantly willing to listen with an open ear. Perhaps you have a gift for gardening, writing, or joking. They are the same things that give you a sense of dignity, therefore honor them. You could even write them on a memo pad and post them daily on your bathroom mirror.

HSPs can also concentrate intensely and take pleasure in becoming lost in their thoughts. Because of this, you will be in an excellent position to succeed in times of intense work.

Be forgiving.

Lastly, we must forgive ourselves for our previous transgressions. Shame, regret, and guilt all work against your capacity to appreciate and value yourself. While HSPs typically find it easier to forgive others, they must also practice self-compassion.

Chapter 4. The Keys to Effective HSP Communication

Highly sensitive individuals have a lot to offer the world. They are intuitive and have the ability to notice minor differences in situations. They cry as much as they laugh, and they can hear the symphony in complete silence. A common source of frustration for many HSPs, however, is the inability to communicate their experiences and demands adequately.

Different communication styles can be described for both HSPs and non-HSPs. However, the four communication styles that people are most likely to utilize at any given time can be summarized as follows:

Aggressive: An aggressive communicator prioritizes their own needs above all else, placing others second. They have a proclivity to be impatient and abrupt. The following are some common statements used by aggressives:

- What led you to believe that would work?
- Why would I go out of my way to help you?
- What do you consider yourself to be?

On the plus side, they are usually successful in meeting their objectives. Setting boundaries is not a problem for someone of this temperament. The only problem is that by dismissing the needs of others and demeaning their point of view, it causes relationships to deteriorate further.

It is worth noting that very few highly sensitive people communicate in an aggressive manner. HSPs do, however, seem to attract those who share their values.

Passive: A passive communicator is the polar opposite of an aggressive communicator. They put others' needs before their own, even if it means putting their own needs last. They have a tendency to come across as ambiguous, unclear and permissive. This type of communication is where the idea of a "yes" man or woman originated. Here are some examples of what they might say.

- "I can't decide...what do you think?"
- "Yeah, I can handle that for you."
- "That's not really my area, but I guess I can help."

The advantage of being in this group is that they can maintain relationships with others relatively easily. What person wouldn't want someone who can meet their wants and needs on the spur of the moment? Inauthenticity, on the other hand, diminishes the significance of those relationships.
If they never say 'no,' their 'yes' means nothing.

Passive-Aggressive: These individuals are wolves dressed as sheep. They promise to do something to make you happy, but then they don't follow through. They insult you, but they do so in a passive voice and with passive language. Alternatively, nonverbal aggression can be used. These are the people who are enraged, but who aren't expressing their feelings. This type of communicator might do any of the following:

- Pretend they are "fine" (even if their tone indicates otherwise)
- Make malicious or spiteful remarks in a non-aggressive manner
- Sulk in silence rather than explain what they need

This group is typically a mixture of personalities. Despite their failure to follow through on the very thing they promised to do, they maintain an appearance of being helpful and considerate. They only go so far as to avoid conflict and meet one's needs, but they don't go far enough to promote healthy communication and personal growth.

Assertive: This is the communication style that everyone strives for. Someone who is assertive is able to balance the needs of others with their own desires in an equal amount of time and space. They say exactly what they mean, and they do so without being defensive. It is their responsibility to advocate for themselves, but they do so in a manner that is respectful of those around them.

Statements of this in action include:

- "I'm having a difficult time with something. I'd like to speak with you about it further. Can we arrange a meeting?"
- "I wish I could assist you, but I am unable to because I have already made other plans."
- "Could you please do me a huge favor? I'm having a hard time getting everything completed. If you have a moment, I would greatly appreciate it if you could assist me."

This group manages to meet their own needs while also taking into consideration the needs of others. If they are able to assist and express a willingness to do so, they will. If they are unable to assist, they will not claim to be able to do so and then duck the question later. There is no ambiguity about their wants or needs, and there is no ambiguity about their ability to meet yours.

Assertiveness Techniques

When someone is overly sensitive, it can be difficult to stand up for their rights and principles in a calm and constructive way. However, it is not uncommon. Some people may speak over them and disregard their feelings and points of view because of their reserved demeanor. Given their vulnerability to being hurt, HSPs despise aggressive communication, and many would rather avoid conflict altogether in the hope that the situation would resolve itself.

While HSPs struggle with conflict and are frequently stepped on by others, I've come to realize that this does not prevent them from being assertive in certain situations. Managing your emotions, setting boundaries, and communicating your thoughts and feelings are all skills that can be developed. The following are strategies to assist in becoming more assertive:

1. Communicate through assertive writing.

Whenever I'm dealing with a conflict, I find it extremely beneficial to communicate the issues in written form. In addition to providing immediate cathartic release, it also helps to clarify the situation and is a useful tool for open communication when used properly. Use of the phrase "I feel" statements when writing about a disagreement with someone is critical when writing a letter about your disagreement. These statements are significant because they frame the situation in a way that reflects your point of view and emotional needs without placing direct blame on the other party.

An assertive letter should be as succinct as possible in explaining the situation, without going into unnecessary detail about the individual. Here's a template you can use to get started:

Greetings,

While bringing up this subject (conflict/misunderstanding) is difficult for me, I believe that it is necessary to do so (despite my reluctance). I've decided to write you a letter because I believe that writing allows me to express myself more effectively.

Recently, I've been feeling betrayed by someone I care about (insert situation). When (the situation) occurs, I have the impression that I am in control (what emotional need is not met).

My thoughts have recently been drawn to this, and I don't want to ignore it any longer. I'd appreciate it if we could get this resolved as soon as possible, but even if we can't, I just wanted you to be aware of how I'm feeling.

Sincerely,
You

2. Be aware of how you come across to people.

The words a person uses and the way they move can reveal a great deal about themselves. Others may perceive an HSPs' humility as a sign of weakness and attempt to take advantage of them because they are overly modest in their own eyes. Certain phrases and words should be avoided if you want to come across as more assertive. Here are some examples:

- **Using the word "just."** A statement's impact is diminished when you use the word "just" because it gives the impression that you're being overly defensive.
- **"I'm not" statements.** It's common for people to say things like "I'm not an expert, but..." in attempt to avoid sounding aggressive or arrogant, but doing so damages the validity of their message.
- **"I can't..." statements.** By starting a statement with "I cant'..." you are implying that you have lost control over your actions by using passive phrasing.
- **Answering with a question.** Saying things like "What if we gave it a shot...?" in a question-and-answer format invites counter-arguments is taken less seriously than a straightforward statement of an idea.
- **Apology statements.** Saying statements like "I apologize for any inconvenience this may have caused you." indicates that you are apologizing for things you have no control over, you come out as untrustworthy and unsure of yourself.
- **Overly emphatic punctuation.** Consider the following text response: "Thanks a lot for your help! ; " In this example, the overuse of exclamation points and emoticons in written or text messages shows that you're self-conscious and worried about being seen as generous.

Another thing to keep in mind is that defensiveness and lack of confidence can be communicated by body language such as folded arms, hunched shoulders, and no eye contact. Speaking before a crowd is a great method to hone your body language. For confidence and stage presence, consider joining a public speaking club or practicing in front of a camera on a regular basis.

3. Don't take everything personally.

Remember that when people are unable to deal with their own problems, they tend to transfer their negativity onto others. This realization will assist you in developing a filter and being less sensitive to others' feelings. It is also important to make an effort to comprehend why you become defensive in certain situations and recognize that taking things personally can give certain individuals more power over you than they should have in the situation. Ultimately, no one has the authority to make you feel inferior without your consent.

4. Take charge of your own happiness and well-being.

It's important to realize that your happiness is not dependent on the happiness of others. Many HSPs are unhappy because they care too much about what others think of them, need their approval, and don't give themselves enough time to relax and breathe.

5. Consider yourself to be equal to others.

There is a possibility that HSPs feel inferior to others, which can have a bad impact on their work and personal relationships.

It's crucial to keep in mind that other people have insecurities, too, even if they don't show them. While we all face the same challenges, our attitudes toward life and relationships with ourselves shape how we see and treat the world around us. Instead of focusing on what others think of you, focus on how you see yourself.

6. Give yourself some time to think through your responses.

Instead of saying what you think people want to hear, say what they require hearing. When it comes to honesty, HSPs can be put into a difficult position.

Don't feel like going out to dinner tonight? Let your friend know exactly how you feel. Before blurting out anything that will be positively welcomed by others, take your time and think it out. Ask yourself, "Is this really what I want to say or do?" before responding.

Perhaps you want to order out and don't feel like getting ready. If this is the case, consider your answer to the other person until you have reformulated it in your head, then respond affirmatively.

7. Speak up if you've been treated unfairly by others.

Keep your guard up and don't let anyone treat you the way they want without your consent. HSPs, by nature, want to please others, so this is a difficult notion for them to grasp. When it comes to other people's feelings, they are overly cautious about speaking out for themselves.

Check to see if you have enough self-respect to confront someone about anything they did to you. A respectful chat with another person can be had even if the topic of discourse is unpleasant. Taking the effort to speak with someone and let them know they'd insulted you can help you become more aggressive in the future.

8. Act confident, even if you don't feel like it.

It's true what they say: "fake it 'til you make it." This is applicable in this case. Even if you don't feel like it, start moving confidently anyhow, and your brain will believe you do. Falsifying your self-confidence may help you succeed in your profession since it makes you appear competent, and employers only care about what they can see on the surface of someone's personality.

Increasing self-esteem and assertiveness in HSPs is feasible if they appear confident in other areas of their life. Relationships are a good example of this.

Highly sensitive people have an uncanny ability to see and understand the emotions and motives of those around them. In fact, they become so focused on others' needs that they forget about their own. At least in part, this problem can be attributed to their desire to avoid upsetting others. As a result, HSPs are more likely to suffer from burnout or be exploited.

HSPs possess unique abilities that they are willing to share with others. However, you must first and foremost be your best self, and this includes being self-assured and genuine to who you are.

Conflict and the Highly Sensitive

Conflict is something that no one enjoys. Highly sensitive people can even appear to be physically harmed by it. With this in mind, highly sensitive people frequently exhibit specific brain patterns during conflict that encourage them to agree as if their lives depended on it. Attempting to keep others happy while also avoiding conflict is a powerful temptation that can be difficult to resist.

But what is the real danger in this behavior? Typically, problems arise only when your needs are in direct conflict with the perceptions of the needs of those you care about. A few examples include the following:

- You want to feel connected to your significant other...but they are longing for some alone time as well. What are you supposed to do?
- You really want to eat right now, but have plans to go to dinner with some friends and they're not quite ready yet. Is it better for you to wait to eat?
- You're desperate for some peace and quiet, but you're just been invited to a group gathering, and the people who invited you are insistent that you attend.

Communicating passively (or passive aggressively) ultimately causes a halt in the flow of your interpersonal interactions. It doesn't matter how hard they try, your friends and family will never be able to read your mind and figure out what you need. And when they don't do what you expect them to, it's insulting. If you erupt in anger, you cause far more problems than if you had just said what you were thinking at the time.

High sensitivity individuals are often natural givers in their relationships, and the cycle of overgiving and underreceiving contributes to the accumulation of resentment in the relationship. For highly sensitive people, giving up on their own needs is one of the worst things they can do in a relationship, and it is one of the most damaging things they can do. If you're an HSP living with a non-HSP partner, you should know that unless you explain your needs clearly, they won't be aware of them. If you've spent your entire life serving others, it's possible you've forgotten about your own needs.

The HSP and Interpersonal Relationships

Is it difficult to meet new people and create friends? Do you ever feel that you're all by yourself, even while you're surrounded by others? It's not uncommon to wish you had the ability to instantly build a stronger bond with another person. The process of making friends when you're a highly sensitive person can be both challenging and stressful.

Perhaps you are overstimulated in a crowded environment. Perhaps it's because of the lack of conversation that you feel so isolated and worn out. Individuals with high levels of sensitivity tend to be introverted and tire easily from listening to small talk. Because of this, finding friends as a sensitive person can be a tiring endeavor. You could only expend so much energy making new people feel at ease. Or you may desire a deeper connection that entails far more than a brief conversation.

Being highly sensitive, you do not have a combative mindset and may experience social discomfort. As a result, highly sensitive people also struggle to deal with verbal aggression due to their caring, compassionate nature. When it comes to social situations, you know what it's like to feel anxious. Highly sensitive individuals are prone to anxiety and the desire to mentally prepare for any situation, including socializing. You must, however, be prepared for the unexpected. Highly sensitive people are more prone to social anxiety as a result of the stress caused by anticipating anger or rejection. Here are some strategies for building relationships with people when you are extremely sensitive:

1. Be picky about who you let into your inner circle. HSPs are sensitive to their surroundings and to other people's emotions. As a result, you may find someone's energy particularly exhausting. Choose the people you let into your life with care:

- Choose those who will help you rather than hurt you.
- Keep in mind that deep friendships are formed in excess of quantity from quality.
- Find people who make you happy and understandable.

2. Don't wallow in self-pity. We've all experienced the moment when we make a mistake or say something incorrectly and spiral into a vicious cycle of negative self-talk. Instead of blaming yourself, practice self-compassion.

Remember the following:

- The people you meet are also human beings who make mistakes.
- You make every effort to connect with your best.
- You have the fortitude to recover from an error.

3. Allow yourself to be vulnerable. We have a tendency to wait for someone else to be vulnerable before we take action ourselves. However, we can also lead by being vulnerable. Express how you feel or what's on your mind when you develop a new connection with someone. People who are vulnerable may find it easier to relate to their human emotions and experiences. Conducting a vulnerability exercise may encourage others to open up and become vulnerable with you. Try any of the following:

- When asked the standard "How are you?" try to be as honest as possible. The bank and grocery checkout line aren't the only places where this applies. Be open and responsive with those who actually care about knowing your state of being, such as your close family and friends. Simple statements like, "I'm fine, although I've been stressed about x this week" are sufficient.

- Be honest about your challenges, but only tell the truth to people you can rely on to listen and offer support.

- If someone says something that hurts or offends you accidentally, say something about it. Defend yourself. Don't let your hurt linger by keeping it bottled up.

4. Modify your questions. Ask open-ended questions to help you get beyond the surface. Try to take the initiative and ask questions to demonstrate to the other person that you are interested and eager to learn more. Here are some examples:

- "What was the most difficult aspect of your experience?"
- "Is there a situation or problem you've recently overcome?"
- "What do you consider to be your greatest achievement in life so far?"
- "What things made you feel great this week?"

5. Relax and enjoy the process. Accept that you might not be able to connect with everyone on a deep level. Some people will put up a barrier or even drain your energy from negativity. Instead of getting to know everyone intimately, savor the pleasure of getting to know someone new.

6. Get out of your own head and into the real world. When we're stuck in our heads, we construct a self-fulfilling prophecy that keeps us from making new acquaintances.

The ability to feel more connected and content comes from building greater relationships with people. However, the most essential thing is that you're having fun while. As a highly sensitive person, you may overthink how you respond with circumstances in an attempt to win friends. When we overthink things, we become entrapped in our minds and miss out on the current moment.

7. Accept that humans have a basic yearning for connection and understanding. People wish to feel a part of something larger than themselves. Make an effort to engage others in conversation and show that you are genuinely interested in what they have to say. Consider ending a relationship if it drains you instead of energizing you. Don't worry about how many connections you have; focus on how good they are. Above everything, stay true to yourself.

How an HSP Can Create Meaningful Connection

Many HSPs feel that they struggle to bridge a meaningful connection with those they want to get close to, whether it be a love interest, potential friend or new co-worker. However, this can be resolved through by reframing how you approach connections.

First, you must determine whether you truly want to connect with the individual. As a highly sensitive person, you may believe that you should connect with someone even if there is a part of you that does not want to connect. You may be hiding certain feelings, or the relationship may not be worth the effort. Take the time to ask yourself if you truly want to develop your relationship and why. Thinking in this manner enables us to form honest relationships, which are essential for highly sensitive people.

The next step when communicating is to make strong eye contact. Fixing on the floor or ceiling will almost certainly result in further disconnect. It's so easy to get lost in your head when you look at something other than the person in front of you. Make careful eye contact so that you can cope with the other person's fear, harm, or vulnerability while they are present.

Approach the relationship with real interest and concern for the other person. Many people with high levels of sensitivity have an innate ability to empathize, but if we're feeling alienated, we may reject it. When we're hurt, our bodies' defenses go into high gear. However, it's possible that the other individual has the same impression. Humility and a sincere desire to understand and empathize with another person can go a long way in building bridges and improving relationships. Keep an open mind and be receptive to the other person's perspective. You can follow through by making time to engage in hobbies together.

If for any reason you create tension with another person, you must accept responsibility. As humans, we can sometimes build walls without even realizing it. We become self-righteous and defensive, blaming others. The connection is formed by both parties who have a duty to expand the relationship. As an HSP, allow this to be a part of both your inner work and any discourse. Take action and let this person know you want to connect with them. Always remember-- connection with people who are different than you does not have to be as difficult if you know how to use your sensitivity to your advantage.

Embrace Your Viewpoint With Others

Being able to connect allows you to lift others and make yourself more cheerful. The more you define yourself as a friend, the less you rely on how others perceive you. Whether or not a social encounter yields a positive outcome, you can be satisfied with your positive contribution. Think of your common ground with others as a common ground for all humanity, rather than one based on culture.

That being said, it is important to recognize that you will not always be able to get what you want. Whether you are regarded a failure or not has nothing to do with whether or not you are popular. The terms "inclusiveness" and "friendliness" should not be used interchangeably with "openness to all." Many people perceive modesty or kindness as flaws, and you may not be able to change that perception. It may be difficult if your values differ significantly from those of those closest to you — a problem that can be solved by implementing healthy stress-relief strategies. Therapy is frequently required in difficult family situations that have persisted for a long time.

Be cautious about your involvements where differences can occur. When you work in a job that is stressful due to political fighting and significant rivalry, you should look for roles that are easy to play and will allow you to be at ease in social situations. A highly sensitive individual can be a great source of information. Emphasize your strengths to reduce or neutralize the group's perception of you as different, which will help you fit in.

A fundamental shift in human consciousness is taking place right now, but it will take time to complete. HSPs are frequently involved in the transition process, despite the fact that it is difficult work. Respecting oneself for one's efforts is essential for HSPs. It is absolutely necessary to take care of your health and implement stress-reduction measures in order to be a productive member of society. A low-stress life can be maintained by taking the long view, managing your expectations, being a good friend to yourself and others, and practicing effective self-care.

Chapter 5. Thriving As An HSP in the Workplace

People who are extremely sensitive to stimuli have a difficult time at work. While high sensitivity people account for about 15 to 20% of the population, they are not uncommon; in fact, nearly every workplace has one or more. As a result, very few work environments are designed to assist the highly sensitive in being successful or performing their best work. Furthermore, for some people with high sensitivity, their job is a source of stress and excessive pressure.

Common Workplace Issues and How To Overcome

HSPs and more likely to experience accelerated levels of stress at work than non-HSPs. They have extremely high levels of empathy, as evidenced by their consistent engagement in brain regions associated with mirror neurons, and they are acutely aware of the mental emotions of others—even complete strangers. The people you work with expose you to everyone else's moods, emotions, and tension. If you are an HSP, you may become easily "flooded." Your day could be derailed no matter where in the office or workplace you set foot. It is exhausting to have to pick up on all of the emotional and mental situations of those you interact with on a daily basis.

For most HSPs, learning to control how they absorb emotions is one of the most beneficial things they can do for themselves. This does not imply rejecting the gift of emotion or stopping everything you are doing. Rather, it means prioritizing your own physical and emotional needs over all else, which allows you to be strong when others make a big deal out of your emotions.

In order to be sensitive and conscientious in the workplace, the vast majority of HSPs prioritize the needs of others over their own. They also loathe burdening others with "fussy" requests. The following are common triggers or sticking points most HSPs face on the job. In the time of remote working, some of these may not apply to all of you, but are worth discussing.

Environmental sensitivities disrupt your productivity.

Suppose a coworker walks in wearing a heavy perfume and you are upset for the rest of the day, but you choose to keep your feelings hidden from everyone else. This might seem like a minor issue, but taking the right action will allow you to be more assertive in other areas of your life.

As much as you want to avoid conflict, you should only allow for the irritation to pass if it occurs randomly. If it is occurring enough to distract you from work, you should speak up. Maintain your composure and assertiveness by stating either of the following:

- "I don't mean to cause any conflict, but I am extremely sensitive to fragrances, and your perfume is distracting" or

- "Migraines occur when I am in close proximity to someone who is wearing cologne or perfume, which makes it difficult for me to do my job duties successfully. It would be appreciated if you could avoid wearing this type of perfume to the office."

Also consider speaking with your manager. Be truthful and express your desire for a different work environment.

Similarly, perhaps you find the fluorescent lights are far too bright all around you in the office. They may also flicker, which can be bothersome or even nauseating for someone who is overly sensitive. While it is unlikely that you will be able to change the lighting at your workplace, you may be able to influence the atmosphere. An old-fashioned desk lamp brought in for a cubicle workstation can help improve the atmosphere of your workspace.

Urgent tasks force you to move quickly.

Have you ever had a large project handed to you by your boss with the expectation that it be done by a certain date? Do they, on the other hand, fail to plan projects and then constantly place their staff in the position of firefighter, requiring them to extinguish the flames each and every time? It's a growing problem in the United States today, and as a result, deadlines are constantly pushed and stress is prevalent. This can be quite unpleasant for the HSP.

This is due to the depth of processing performed by HSPs. They take a methodical approach to each assignment and put in significant cognitive effort. Highly sensitive people do their best work, thinking things through as they go along and working more slowly and methodically as a result.

Although you cannot directly manage your boss's work habits or deadlines, you can help meet them indirectly. It is critical to explicitly explain what you need to do to complete a specific assignment. For example, you could say:

> "When you requested that 'A' be delivered by tomorrow, you also requested that 'B' be delivered by the same time. However, there isn't enough time to complete both tasks at the simultaneously. Can you please clarify which is more important?"

You might also consider making your own weekly work plan and presenting it to your boss.

You "soft skills" are undervalued.

HSPs bring a diverse set of skills to the workplace, which only improves it. They pay attention to small details, are concerned about the needs of their team members, and make certain that things are done correctly. Furthermore, they are typically friendly and warm-hearted, making them good office colleagues. Each of these abilities is inextricably linked to the achievement of a company's goals.

Supervisors, on the other hand, frequently overlook this. Companies will hire and promote based on "hard" abilities, even if it means putting the office jerk in charge of a project, rather than looking for applicants who are best suited for a position. Because of your team-oriented attitude, you may be overlooked in your next performance evaluation.

The only way to increase the value of your skills in the workplace is to speak up. To be successful, you must inform your management of your actions so that they can assist you. For instance, you could say the following:

- "We don't know how we'll finish this project on time if we don't have a specific strategy in place. So that we're all on the same page, I made a checklist for us."

Alternatively, you could inform your manager that soft skills can have a significant impact:

- "He's getting a lot of flack from the client because of the way he addresses everyone. It appears to be influencing our image. What are we going to do about it?"

Handling criticism can be challenging.

HSPs are highly sensitive to criticism, and their subsequent emotions are intense. They are willing to sacrifice their own happiness in order to put the needs of others before their own.

Being told you've done something wrong, especially in a professional setting, can be a painful experience. However, it is necessary to process feelings before you can use feedback to improve the situation. Do you believe your boss is aware of your sensitivities? These phrases will assist you in dealing with criticism or a difficult evaluation process:

- "I appreciate your comments, but please be aware that I am extremely sensitive to negative feedback."
- "I understand what you are saying; it's just that I need to think about it for a while."
- "Would you please tell me how I can improve this in the future, as I'd like to do better?"

Provide assurance that you will follow up with them shortly after the meeting.

How to Avoid Overanalyzing at Work

When you are conscientious and driven, it is almost certain that you will consider your circumstances carefully. Nonetheless, many people, particularly highly sensitive people, frequently find themselves preoccupied with too much thought, causing anxiety and stress. As a result, their productivity and creativity suffer. Here's how to avoid hyper-analyzing if you're an HSP at work.

Recognize Unhelpful Thoughts

What thoughts come to mind when you begin to overthink? Nine times out of ten, they are exaggerated depictions of reality.

When it comes to overthinking, cognitive distortions are better known as negative self-talk. Both impulsive and illogical beliefs are examples of cognitive distortions since they feed and prolong negative emotions and keep you trapped in a mental circle. One common distortion is an "all or nothing" mentality. This can appear in the form of an inner dialogue that operates on extremes. An example could be thinking "I have to be perfect, or else I'm a total failure." If you jump to conclusions, you might even think, "He didn't respond to my email, so he must be well aware of my dislike for him".

When cognitive distortions appear, we find it well worth our time to reflect on them and label them. Recognize that this idea is unhelpful, and then take a moment to acknowledge it to yourself. Then, by purposefully reinterpreting these upsetting thoughts, see if you can come up with a more positive statement.

My preferred reframing strategy is known as the "rule of five." When you get stuck in your thoughts, just stop, look at your hand, and come up with five different ways to perceive the situation.

With your fingertips, estimate the various options. Depending on the circumstance, you could ask yourself any of the following:

- What if I knew everything would go smoothly?

- What if I misinterpreted what they were saying?
- What if I didn't have all the facts?
- What if something happened I wasn't aware of to prompt the situation?
- Is the outcome really that important?
- Did I present myself in a way that I wasn't conscious of?

The rule of five can assist you in changing your self-talk, transforming negative statements into neutral or even balanced ones. Rather than succumbing to their old, ingrained response mechanisms, you can approach situations with greater calm by consciously adopting a more compassionate perspective.

Reduce the amount of stimuli in your environment to a bare minimum.

When you're overwhelmed and anxious, it's practically impossible to think rationally. While this is true for everyone, individuals who aim for perfection but are constantly overwhelmed will find this to be certainly the case. Make room in your calendar for extra time to deal with a pressing situation. Take your time before going to a meeting. Allow yourself a 15- to 20-minute recovery period between events on your calendar.

If you are in a managerial role, instead of allowing a "drop-in" approach to co-workers, consider instituting an "office hours" policy. Rather than interrupting you while you are working and causing tension, set a schedule for team members to drop by or schedule time on your calendar.

Find a way to make yourself heard.

If you've tried to silence your own thoughts, you're aware that it's ineffective. It's like trying to hold a beach ball underwater while suppressing your thoughts. No matter how hard you keep the ball submerged, it will eventually reach the surface and make a loud splash. Instead, convert an existing channel into a platform for your creativity.

You may feel overwhelmed at times because you are impacted by your surroundings, yet your intuitive nature also allows you to draw from it when the circumstance calls for it. Many highly sensitive people carry a notebook around with them to capture their rush of ideas on the fly. To help you capture and organize your thoughts, also consider installing a whiteboard in your workspace. Knowing your inner world as a creative person may lead to exciting breakthroughs, fresh solutions to problems, and a particular clarity that most of your coworkers will never get to experience.

How To Avoid Career Stagnation as an HSP

It can sometimes be difficult to find a job that is a good fit for an HSP. A difficult work environment can cause stress, frustration, and overwhelm. Because you are different from others, you are at risk of being overlooked, underappreciated or bullied. Although I am aware of the vulnerability associated with this trait, I truly believe that being extremely sensitive gives us a lot of potential in any profession. We can be successful, but we can also be happy in our jobs if we learn to maximize our abilities.

Without a doubt, highly sensitive people can work in a wide range of professions. However, because HSPs are frequently required to work in stressful, exhausting, and overburdened environments, it can be difficult for some to earn a living.

In many environments there are bullies in the workplace, as well as people with narcissistic tendencies who seek to manipulate and dominate an HSP. Likewise, many HSPs find that their coworkers' outspokenness has drowned out their own voice, making it more difficult to be noticed for promotions.

Working solely for a paycheck does not appeal to you as a sensitive individual, even though you still do it like most people. However, it is most fulfilling when you know that your work is making a positive difference in the lives of others.

Unfortunately, many jobs do not provide this type of benefit. To maximize productivity, the majority of projects include repetitive chores. It can be soul-draining. The worst fate an HSP can imagine is a life devoid of meaning. Here are some ways the highly sensitive can get ahead:

Consider new work assignments.

Even if it is for a professional purpose, learning can be both meaningful and enjoyable. Even if your current position has become obsolete, look for opportunities to take on new or different responsibilities. Despite the fact that you may find it difficult to connect your passion to a career, you will find fulfillment in pursuing it on your own time.

Ensure that you are constantly monitoring your resume.

When you update your résumé, you get a new perspective on your work history and achievements. You share your accomplishments with the world every time you have a positive impact on quality, production, or profit. As a result, it may also assist you in obtaining a better job.

Concentrate on the people around you.

Individuals are the brightest object on an HSPs' radar. If you can connect deeply with your coworkers, you can often create a truly profound, very human sense of meaning – even for the most difficult task.

As simple as these ideas sound, they are important to keep in mind when looking for advancement. Even more important is what you bring to the professional world in terms of natural traits.

How To Maximize Your HSP Gifts in the Workplace

Understanding your personal strengths and needs is critical to maximizing your success. You must first fully know yourself before you can expect people to understand you at work. Do you have a high level of sensitivity and natural talent? What distinguishing qualities do you possess? What piques your interest the most?

Consider the conditions that allow you to do your best work, such as being in silence. Are you satisfied with working on your own? You can only understand your own demands and abilities if you are clear on them within yourself.

Identify what makes you different from others and own it.

Being an HSP distinguishes you from the rest of the population. Many people go to great lengths to fit in, follow trends, and do things the way others do. However, this is completely unjustified.

As an HSP, you're not like most people. Doing things the same way every time or attempting to compare yourself to others will only add to your frustration. Everyone else's perspective on life and the world around you is very different from yours. Furthermore, you have insights into topics that others are not aware of. Be prepared for people who are unfamiliar with your subject matter. They haven't been exposed to the same sensory information as you, so they won't understand. Respecting your differences can lead to a wonderful sense of peace.

Make the most of your attention to details.

Your energy will dwindle if you do not use your unique gifts, talents, and abilities. You're a sensitive person with a variety of talents.

Do you have a special talent for locating information? Is it possible to acquire knowledge without being aware of how or why you obtained it? Do you get a lot of requests for advice or to talk about personal issues? All of these instances allow you to demonstrate that you have unique abilities in the finer details

It's a common misconception that once you've identified your strengths, you have to sit on them. In fact, the opposite is true: you should use your strengths at work, and you can certainly leverage them. It is unusual to find a workplace where problem solving and gaining people's trust are not priorities.

Allot time for self-care routines.

Because it is so easy for HSPs to be overstimulated at work, self-care is critical. Create simple habits to save energy in the mornings, throughout the day, and just before bed. Spend some time alone with yourself. Find a quiet place to go when you're at work, even if it's only for a few minutes. Before or after work, invigorate yourself with something relaxing. Your personal style may be quite distinct, but consider doing things like yoga or relaxing in a hot tub.

Incorporating plants or fresh flowers, for example, is a simple way to bring nature into your workspace. It's incredible how a single beautiful natural element can help an HSP.

Speak up and be assertive using objectivity.

I agree that this can be difficult for people who are overly sensitive. It's especially difficult for introverted, highly sensitive people. It's possible that you're hesitant to express yourself because you've previously been chastised for being different.

As a result, knowing yourself at your most basic level and accepting who you are—fully owning your identity—will lead to increased self-confidence. Now is the time to begin speaking with assertiveness. At work, you have a fantastic opportunity to make your voice heard. Consider talking to your supervisor or someone in management who is open to your suggestions. Strive to be firm without seeming fussy. Focus on the facts only.

Even if people don't immediately jump to your assistance, speaking up can open doors for you that you never expected.

How to Manage the Highly Sensitive

This section is for both the HSP and non-HSP manager who is in the position of overseeing others or is interested in hiring someone who is highly sensitive.

Sensitive people are frequently ranked as the best performers in their organizations when it comes to producing excellent results. Employees and managers form positive working relationships because HSPs are generally well-liked and admired for their thoughtfulness, even if they experience periods of stress from time to time.

We must dispel the widespread misconception that sensitivity is a flaw. The ability to perceive the world more deeply is a gift that, when strategically applied, can inspire creativity, innovation, and career advancement.

If you are a manager, it is your responsibility to ensure that everyone on your team thrives. Here's how to find highly sensitive employees and how to help them realize their full potential if you're looking for them.

According to a 2014 study, people with higher levels of HSP have more blood flow in brain regions associated with emotional processing, awareness, and empathy. Because of their inherent cognitive abilities, HSPs can be emotionally attuned to the needs of others at the expense of their own personal well-being. HSPs are more prone to perfectionism and other people-pleasing tendencies than the general population.

The higher a person's sensitivity to stimulation, the more sensitive they will be to external stimuli. As a result, they may become overwhelmed in stressful situations. Deadlines may overwhelm them, and their reputation for being unprepared for meetings may work against them. Open floor plans in offices have the additional effect of causing HSPs to seek refuge in a private location.

HSPs enjoy researching complex subjects because they are highly perceptive. They enjoy making plans and devising schemes. Coworkers who lack nuance awareness, on the other hand, may frustrate them.

That being said, it's all in a day's work to teach your team members to appreciate their abilities while also providing them with the tools they need to deal with their emotions.

Here are a few pointers to bring out the talents and strengths of the highly sensitive in your team.

- **Consider stress as a topic for discussion.**

Because HSPs internalize their emotions more deeply, they also experience higher levels of stress. As a result, those who are having problems at work may be less willing to speak up for fear of being perceived as weak or incapable. Ask your highly sensitive colleague how they are doing and check in on a regular basis. When you show concern for your employees' well-being, you are not only supporting and appreciating them, but you are also providing a forum for discussion and problem-solving.

- **Optimize their workspace for isolation.**

People who are highly sensitive are prone to feeling overwhelmed, which is why it is necessary to develop systems and habits that will assist them in performing well. While HSPs dislike being watched, they may benefit from solitude in order to focus their full attention on a specific task

- **Criticism must be delivered tactfully.**

An HSP is more sensitive to criticism than others, and they may overcorrect and, in some cases, jeopardize their well-being in order to be liked by others. Delay making comments until you have met with the highly sensitive person on a regular basis. Provide feedback in a calm, even-tempered manner. Allow your HSP employee time to consider their responses before responding immediately. Of course, this is excellent advice for anyone providing feedback, but highly sensitive people will find it especially helpful.

- **Bridge their talents with company goals.**

The HSP is motivated by a desire to believe that their work is significant. They are committed and eager to make a difference. Assist HSPs in being more effective in using their natural empathy, communication, and organizational abilities. An HSP who lacks deep motivation may become apathetic. They deserve your help in connecting their efforts to a larger goal. Managing and leading sensitive individuals requires a steep learning curve, but it is possible to assist your employees in developing their own strengths to help them succeed.

Overall, it appears that HSP awareness in the workplace is growing. It is, however, the HSP's responsibility to learn how to care for themselves. A highly sensitive person can succeed in the workplace, but they must take the initiative. It is critical that they help themselves and inform others on how to help them. And when they do, the rest of the world will realize how incredible they are. My hope is that when the broader community realizes how much they have to offer, they will be accepted and valued. Only when organizations compete for HSPs will they begin to hire more of them.

Chapter 6. Relationships and the Highly Sensitive Person

Being an HSP has an impact on all aspects of our lives and presents a number of challenges in the field of love. This is especially true when it comes to differences in gender.

Overall, HSPs do not conform to the cultural ideals of men and women. In our society, many argue that the ideal male is stoic, domineering, motivated, daring, risky, and physically powerful. The ideal man is not seen as being soft or sensitive. On the other hand, many see the ideal woman as outgoing, caring, flexible, and concerned with her appearance. She addresses and cares about the needs and desires of others more than her own.

While the highly sensitive man (HSM) may be stoic and emotional, he is inherently more sensitive than non-HSMs. Because there is no correlation between HSM and these attributes, HSMs can be physically powerful and motivated. However, due to their sensitivity, the highly sensitive male primarily pauses and reflects before making decisions. This is his nature, so the courageous and risky characteristics of the ideal man are unlikely to be fulfilled. The highly sensitive male is also not typically domineering because they are sensitive to the needs of their partner and, of course, a laid-back personality.

On the contrary, the highly sensitive woman (HSW) closely resembles the cultural ideal. Women, after all, should be sensitive, particularly to the needs and demands of others. However, no matter how introverted a woman is, she cannot be so sensitive that she needs time to herself. The ideal superwoman is more powerful. And the HSW falls short of that standard. Both highly sensitive women and men reach an over-stimulation point much faster than other people, necessitating downtime.

Highly sensitive men and women frequently have lower self-esteem than non-HSPs because they do not meet culture's ideals. This lack of self-esteem has an impact on their relationships, as HSPs frequently suffer from profound gender insecurities.

HSPs and non-HSPs alike frequently regard their less sensitive partners as ideal and are envious of them. If HSPs do not feel good about themselves and believe they are not ideal, their partners will be aware of their lack of self-esteem.

According to research by Dr. Elaine Aron's research, the highly sensitive person's relationships are frequently unhappy. They are more aware of their surroundings and the people within them, so they are more concerned about their spouse's behavior and the potential consequences. They also feel more stressed and require more alone time, which can aggravate the relationship.

Regardless, the highly sensitive trait attracts many non-HSPs despite its difficulties. Non-HSPs value their empathy and compassion. They value the HSP's desire for meaningful, long-term connections and distaste of the flashy and fleeting. It may be a breath of fresh air for someone who has never encountered a highly sensitive individual before to hear them out. People who need their help are also drawn to HSPs because of their open, kind and empathic nature. This appeal, however, can be disappointing. Too often, people are more likely to benefit from their care than to help themselves, and HSPs are more likely to be personal therapists or doormats than equal partners.

Many HSPs experience self-doubt or low self-esteem because they do not always embrace or value their sensitivity. In order to gain approval and affection from a romantic partner who desires their character, they may become even more empathetic, helpful, and sensitive to the feelings of others. Aron's research has discovered a trait known as "mate sensitivity" in extremely sensitive people, or the ability to quickly assess what their partner enjoys. When an HSP is aware of someone's desires, they go out of their way to make them materialize. This cycle tends to repeat itself in an unhealthy manner.

However, if the HSP provides too much, problems may arise. The more they give, the more people will take, until the HSP loses sight of their own needs, resulting in exhaustion, resentment, and unhappiness. At the same time, HSPs are perplexed as to why, after working so hard and blaming themselves, that they are so dissatisfied.

Rather than trying harder to help their partners, HSPs need to learn how to help themselves. Here are some tips:

1. Become acquainted with yourself. Determine what you require first. You can't meet your needs if you don't know what they are.

2. Establish boundaries. In order to protect their sensitivity, HSPs must establish strong, clear statements. It is not egotistical to say 'no' or to express your needs to others. You are simply looking after you. If you're with a safe person, your need for connection, awareness, or comprehension of your own feelings won't make them uncomfortable.

3. Accept yourself. People will learn to accept and respect the HSP if they see you are doing so. If someone says you're "too sensitive" or that you need to change, don't engage in argument. When you are told to "simply relax", then they are not someone you want to be around. Arons' theory is that sensitive individuals are also expressive by nature. There is nothing they can do to hide their feelings, whether it's fear, rage, or sheer joy. Both you and your spouse must be valued and accepted if you are to succeed. HSPs can be difficult to grasp for some non-HSPs, but those who care about you will make an effort to appreciate your uniqueness and try to understand it. Sensitivity is a gift that should be developed and enjoyed rather than hidden or corrected. You are the first to nurture it.

4. Take a stand for yourself. HSPs dislike conflict and often avoid it rather than face it, which means that instead of standing up for themselves, they devote all of their energy to soothing and placating their spouse. Aron adds that sensitive people may feel torn between speaking up and remaining silent for fear of eliciting negative reactions from others. Disagreement, on the other hand, must not be confrontational. You should express your beliefs calmly and openly while also requesting that your partner follow your lead in doing the same. Accept your role in the conflict and apologize if you are incorrect. If things become heated, take a break and go for a walk until everyone has calmed down.

5. Be accountable. It is up to you to satisfy your own desires, which may differ greatly from those of your partner. Many people focus too much on themselves, whereas HSPs frequently focus too much on others. Taking responsibility for our lives is the key to a successful partnership. You should treat yourself with the same love and kindness that you do your partner.

6. Be wary of energy vampires. For some people, learning or helping themselves is not an option, therefore they want you to do it for them instead. This isn't good for an HSP, unfortunately. It's like a drowning man trying to save himself by dragging you down with him. It is best to recognize when you are being taken advantage of and set appropriate boundaries. This is covered in more detail in the next chapter.

7. You must be able to heal yourself first. We sometimes need to take time before we finish a relationship to heal ourselves from previous experiences that have harmed our feelings. Our own anxieties and insecurities frequently exacerbate our relationship's problems. And we can learn how to grow in a relationship if our partner encourages us and wants us to develop and heal.

8. Do not behave like a bailiff. Even though it's hard to watch someone you care about suffer through life, you have no priority to feel sorry for them. You must take care of yourself if you want to be who you truly are and achieve your potential. The only way others learn to walk on their own is to trip and fall. Then brush themselves off and try again. You always have the option to offer mercy, but sometimes you just have to step back and allow things work themselves out on their own accord.

9. Don't be a pain in the neck. If your partner doesn't love you or understand you, don't make an effort to change that. Regardless of what people say, trust their actions. Don't linger if you don't feel loved. If you don't know what they need, be there for them, but give them an opportunity to change.

10. Show compassion to yourself. Similar to the third point discussed, when you value and appreciate yourself, you make time for your inner child and treat him or her with respect. However, it's not a guarantee that you'll fall more in love with another person as a result. But the truth is, you don't have to rely on other people for the affection you need and want. When you take care of yourself, you are able to contribute to others without having to make any sacrifices in return. Because you fill your own reservoir with love, you can freely and generously give to others.

Healthy relationships for a highly sensitive person can only be achieved by giving more to yourself than you do to others. A good and loving relationship can develop between HSPs and non-HSPs if both partners have enough esteem to ensure their own needs are met.

Couples in Distress

As a therapist, it was always surprising to me how many men told me they were happy in their relationship but their wife wasn't. This usually starts years before, but they're in the room with me because the wife has stated that she wants to be separated from her husband or divorce him. The male is frequently in a state of disarray and had no idea that things were so bad for her. It was heartbreaking because I kept seeing the same trend. I wish I could go back in time and give them the skills they needed sooner.

Many women have been socialized to believe that minimizing or ignoring their own needs is a selfless act of generosity. Perhaps they give up going to the gym or a favorite class, meeting up with friends, or enjoying "me" time that they used to enjoy in order to focus on the ever-growing to-do list at home, but the husband continues to participate in golf or basketball tournaments with his friends on the weekends. During this stage, resentment frequently begins to simmer.

Based on what I've learned from my observations, highly sensitive women tend to undertake most of the domestic and childcare duties, even if they have full-time jobs outside the home. Along with grocery shopping and cooking, they coordinate the children's extracurricular activities, drive them to doctor's appointments, and oversee the family as a whole. They're frequently in charge of planning parties, weddings, and other social gatherings. Since it is impossible to get everything done in a single day, resentment will start to build up. The onset of larger problems can occur years before the onset of smaller problems. When we are depleted or have unmet needs, we are more likely to become resentful.

As the resentment tank fills up, disconnect begins to occur, and once this happens, intimacy frequently begins to wane or disappear entirely. This is the point at which the male partner frequently begins to build his own tank of resentment, which manifests itself in the form of anger, depression, disconnect, or even infidelity. Conflicts that didn't bother you before start to trouble you more frequently each day. That towel or pair of socks that was left on the floor has now become a major issue rather than a minor inconvenience. When the conflict escalates or negative external behaviors become more prevalent, some individuals turn to alcohol or drugs, which only serves to exacerbate the situation.

If there are children involved, it is natural for them to have emotional difficulties such as anxiety or sadness when their parent's relationship and the home degrade over time. This is where counseling comes into play. When a child starts having issues at school or shows signs of anxiety or despair, it's critical to get help immediately. For the most part, couples will first look for support for their children before seeking counseling in their marriage.

As a result of the complexity of separating children and ongoing living expenditures, many people find themselves stuck in this stage for years. It is highly recommended that you seek professional help from a therapist if you recognize yourself in any of these stages. It is best to work with a therapist who is well-versed in the high sensitivity personality trait and who can guide you through the process of discovering your needs and how to express them.

HSP Traits That Create Conflict in a Relationship

Without a doubt, many non-HSPs find it difficult to comprehend the differences between themselves and their HSP partner, which can result in conflict. The characteristics listed below are the most frequently encountered sources of conflict. In the section that follows, you will learn how to overcome these differences in order to improve your relationship.

HSPs need more downtime than their partners.

Because HSPs have more sensitive neurological systems and analyze subtleties more deeply, their nervous systems are significantly more accelerated than non-HSPs. This is why they need adequate downtime, which allows them to recharge and return to the world in top form. If HSPs are not sufficiently recovered, they may become irritated, agitated, and even depressed.

Downtime is a physiological requirement, much like water. Given the lower ideal excitement level of HSPs, the degree of stimulation can be a problem if an HSP is partnered with a non-HSP.

In contrast, non-HSPs, can spend an entire day shopping at the mall, meet with friends right after supper, and then go to a party – all without pausing. That, of course, appears normal to them. HSPs, on the other hand, would find such a combination of activities too taxing. After a long day of shopping, you might need a short break. If you're too tired from all the stimulation in the mall, you might have to call it a day and stay at home until you get to bed.

A non-HSP spouse may feel abandoned by the HSP as a result of this temperament clash. The non-HSP may have to experience the world without its spouse on occasion. With all this being said, both couples can benefit from the HSP's need for rest and frequent downtime.

HSPs dislike confrontation.

HSPs frequently avoid confronting their spouses when something bothers them. They want as much peace and harmony as possible because fighting is too stressful. They don't want to be overwhelmed, and even a minor difference can cause an HSP to become frazzled.

Because of their caring characteristics, HSPs will do anything with a partner for a long time without complaining. Even if they despise cooking, they can cook a supper for every night when their spouse gets home from work. A non-HSP will never know because they'll never tell them. It's not that they're dishonest; they just don't want to be overwhelmed by confrontation.

The main issue with HSPs who avoid confrontation is that they allow resentment to grow. HSPs may resent their relationships, especially if they keep them for too long.

HSPs are sensitive to minor details.

Because HSPs are naturally attuned to subtleties, they can easily detect the complexities of their partners' actions and words. They notice and assess the smallest of changes in behavior. As a result, HSPs perceive things that their partners are unaware of and feel intensely about things that their partners might not know about themselves.

A typical scenario for an HSP is that they feel a small shift in their relationship – for example, a slight difference in how they and their partner communicate – but the partner has no idea that HSP feels intense emotions. Because of this disdain for confrontation, the HSP often fights alone, and this creates internal resistance in the harmony of the relationship. HSPs may falsely consider their connections to be satisfactory because they are conscientious. They want to ensure that they meet their lovers' needs and desires, but they can become restless and insufficient as lovers if they have to fulfill every need and desire of their partners. Because they are the most attentive one, they can easily become overwhelmed by their partners' sentiments and actions.

As an HSP, it is critical that you do not lose sight of your role in a not-so-sensitive society as someone who does not fit the ideal of a man or a woman. As HSPs, you carry a lot of good, and in our violent society, you are more gentle, thoughtful, and aware way of being is needed.

It is critical that you do not envy your partner and lose sight of the benefits you bring to your relationship as an HSP. You will most likely bring more careful thought and tranquility to your relationship and inspire your lover to take better care of themselves. As an HSP, your romantic love can work wonderfully as long as you accept, accommodate, and recognize that no relationship is perfect.

How to Overcome HSP Trait Conflict

Maybe you're bored by the lack of deep connection or resentful because your partner isn't adapting to your needs. Maybe you find yourself exhausted by the obligation to maintain a full social schedule, or overstimulated by the noise of your relationship. This is a common experience for highly sensitive people, regardless of whether they are with another HSP or someone who is not. You tend to attract superstar partners because you have an innate proclivity to be more empathic and notice minute details such as nonverbal cues. However, because you tend to prioritize others and avoid conflict, your connections are not always welcomed and encouraged. Being more focused on how you manage your relationship can make a significant difference in you life.

Be more direct.

You may need to be more direct in order to satisfy your desires while responding to the needs of others. Being highly sensitive, you are able to detect minute changes in body language or voice tones and have a keen sense of intuition that helps you to anticipate others' needs before they are expressed. Of course, you want your partner to be as attentive as you are.

Unfortunately, a non-HSP spouse may fall short of your expectations because his or her brain is not as perceptive as yours, or because your HSP companion is overburdened. This is why you must be more direct in expressing your desires. Think of it like making your voice louder. It is critical that your spouse succeeds by clearly expressing your needs. When partners fail to respond to your "connection requests" on a regular basis, resentment develops and your relationship becomes estranged.

Make time for yourself.

Because HSPs have competing demands, finding the right balance of time and quality moments with your spouse can be extremely difficult. But if you don't prioritize on your own, you will become overstimulated, which leads to impatience, anxiety and stress. It is beneficial to develop a consistent downtime schedule, such as making time for yourself right after work or organizing a self-care day once a week.

Allow for differences with your partner.

After spending time working with pairs, I frequently encountered tension due to differences in empathy and emotional sensitivity. As an HSP, you anticipate that everyone else will have similar requirements or routines as you do.

Whether or not the two partners are extremely sensitive, it is critical to recognize that differences in preferences and sensitivity will occur. When both spouses are HSPs, one may be extremely sensitive to light, while the other may be less disturbed but extremely sensitive to loud noises. A person's personality traits and life experiences can mix in so many different ways that two people will always be at odds. This can be overcome by avoiding jumping to conclusions about your partner and by asking for their point of view instead.

Take Breaks from Conflict or Arguments

Conflict is a major issue for highly sensitive people because they are frequently overstimulated and move more quickly into combat or flight mode. When this occurs, you or your partner will begin expressing your anger (fight) or leaving the area (flight). HSPs are frequently the first to call a truce due to the intensity of emotional and physical discomfort caused by conflict. Ending the conflict provides a temporary solution, but it does not rule out the possibility of the conflict reoccurring, which becomes the ultimate destroyer of relationships.

When you're both comfortable, come up with a strategy for dealing with disagreements. What are the ground rules for communicating with one another, taking breaks, and nonverbally communicating your needs when you're overwhelmed by emotion? By having established conflict guidelines, the HSP partner will make it easier to navigate the discomfort of fighting.

Make intentional connections and shared experiences.

Highly sensitive people become bored quickly, feel misunderstood, and are vulnerable to emotional pain when there is no meaningful connection in their relationship. With so many demands on our time and attention, it's easy to overlook the importance of your partner's connection while attending to your own. HSPs are frequently too overwhelmed to take care of everything.

Unfortunately, if you do not actively engage with your partner, the relationship begins to deteriorate and becomes more vulnerable to stress and conflict. "If you do not begin with a profound understanding of each other, your marriage can easily lose its direction if your lives change so briefly and drastically," says Dr. John Gottman in *The Seven Principles for the Making Marriage Work.*

It is critical for HSPs to prioritize what is most important and to set strict limits on your limited connectivity capacity. Schedule a date with your partner for a specific night or day of the week. Take advantage of this time for pleasure, and then spend some time conversing, perhaps over dinner or on a long, uninterrupted walk. Simply listen with curiosity and for an extended period of time. Learn about your partner's inner life (their fears, hopes, objectives, and joys) and what happened in their life during last week. As simple as it sounds, when partners share common experiences, they form a strong bond.

Celebrate Your Collective Conscious

As humans, our "negative bias" tends to focus on what goes wrong rather than what works well. This is an intelligent survival strategy, but HSPs get caught up in it and forget about the good things around them. Tackling the issues increases your partner's rage while also improving your emotional and physical health as a highly sensitive person.

My favorite method for improving positive thinking in a partnership is to create a shared notebook of gratitude in which you record your accomplishments and what you enjoyed about the previous week. Then, take a few moments to read and appreciate what each of you has written.

To be happy and engaged in a relationship, highly sensitive people must find a balance of calm duty and meaningful shared experiences with their partners. To meet these expectations, you may need to be direct with your spouse and accept if their tastes differ. Highly sensitive people thrive in all areas when your interactions are balanced and mutually beneficial.

Using the Speaker - Listener Method With Your Partner

Another excellent tool for better communication comes from the Gottman Method, which has been the subject of decades of research into couples' therapy.

Communicating with the speaker-listener method is quite effective. People with high levels of sensitivity can benefit greatly from this strategy. Each participant has the same amount of time to talk and listen. When this happens, the listener takes notes while they listen, which keeps emotional dialogues on course since writing engages the cognitive brain and prevents the emotional brain from gaining control of the conversation. Rules and expectations affect both the speaker and the listener. The ultimate goal is for everyone to be able to express themselves and be heard and understood at the same time.

The listener's body language is extremely important. Your listening skills are being undermined if you are rolling your eyes or interrupting others. If you and your partner are both able to communicate calmly with one another, you may be able to complete some of these steps on your own. In the event that volatility or your emotional brain takes control, working with a therapist will be easier and more productive.

Keeping your cool is key to this method being beneficial for both parties. The listener will have a harder time understanding what you are saying if you are agitated or emotional while speaking. If you are the listener and you are upset, it will be difficult to listen objectively. So your first order of business is to take care of yourself in order to remain calm.

Here is the order of communication when you agree to sit down with your partner for a discussion.

<u>Steps for The Speaker</u>

1. Tell the story of what you're going through and express your feelings by using "I" statements. Keep the word "you" from being used as a sentence opener whenever possible. Doing so results in defensiveness and you will not be heard. A better approach is for the speaker to express something like "I have been feeling detached recently, and that makes me sad," rather than something like "you always make me feel sad..."

2. Remain objective and stick to the facts.

In the second step, it is imperative to stay on the topic of discussion. The region of the brain capable of processing new information is shut down when someone is angry, extremely emotional, or defensive. You can only have fruitful discussions if you are relaxed.

Blame statements only serve to make the listener more defensive. The words 'always' and 'never' should be avoided as well, as this is a blame statement that will almost certainly provoke contention, and as a result, you will not be understood.

Avoid negative or "blame" statements such as the following:

- "You always go out with your friends, but I never get to go out with my friends."
- "When I heard you mention (insert incident or fact), I felt (insert reaction or response)."
- "When I watch you going out every weekend with your friends and I am trapped at home with the kids by myself, I feel bitterness developing inside of me."

Take this opportunity to rephrase the circumstance that led to the discussion. This will serve as a clarification to the listener. Examples include:

- "I have been missing time with friends due to the burden of household responsibilities."
- "I feel like I don't have enough downtime to relax."
- "I feel like I have no one to converse with about my struggles at work."

3. Identify a positive need that you have.

The majority of us complain rather than express our needs, which usually results in defensiveness. Empathy is elicited by stating a positive need. In this step, indicate what you require, but frame it in a positive light. Here is a comprehensive of common statements:

- I'm in desperate need of a hug.
- I'm in desperate need of some alone time.
- I need more help with household chores, and I was hoping we could spread them more evenly between us.
- I require additional assistance with the children and would like to discuss this with you in order to determine what would be most beneficial for me.
- My request is that we sit down and discuss our schedules to figure out how we can spend more quality time together in the near future.
- I think you and I should see a couple's therapist together so that I can talk about what has been bothering me and we can come up with a solution.
- I require your assistance in putting the children to bed at night so that I can have some "me" time to rest and recuperate.
- I need some assistance getting the kids ready in the mornings, and I'd like to sit down with you and figure out a way to divide up the work so that it's less chaotic for me in the mornings.
- Spending more time together, such as going on a date or doing some of the fun things we used to do, will help us reconnect.
- Making a family schedule, in my opinion, will make us feel more organized."

Steps for the Listener

1. Identify the speaker's personal narrative. Respond in a non-judgmental manner to what you heard them say. You should refrain from adding your own content or attempting to fix anything at this time. During this stage, you are only listening to the conversation.

2. Identify the emotional state of the speaker. It is beneficial for them to express their feelings, and if they did not tell you, you should inquire.

3. Recognize and validate the speaker's feelings. You are not required to agree with them in order to validate them. You are confirming that they are having this emotional reaction to something. The phrase "It makes sense that you feel..." can be used to begin the validation process.

4. Identify the speaker's positive need. What are they trying to express? If you're not sure, you can always ask them, "What is your positive need?"

5. Confirm if they need anything else. Ask them if they feel heard and if they have anything else to add. "Do you think I covered everything, or is there anything you think I missed or that you need me to explain more clearly?"

It takes some practice to master this speaker-listener technique, but once you do, it is powerful. It has been my experience that couples who have been arguing for years are finally able to communicate after utilizing this strategy. It's incredible, and you can use it for any discussion you want. Ultimately, we all want to be understood and heard.

Highly sensitive people must strike a balance between quiet moments for themselves and meaningful shared activities with their partners if they are to feel content and connected in their relationships. In order to have these requirements addressed, we may need to be direct with our spouse and understand that their choices may differ from ours in certain situations. People who are highly sensitive will prosper in all areas of their lives when their relationships are balanced and mutually helpful.

Chapter 7. The Power of Setting Boundaries

Being an HSP, like anything else, has its advantages and disadvantages. Extremely sensitive people have an exceptionally strong intuitive and empathic connection with others. Unfortunately, when this occurs, people-pleasing and a disregard for personal boundaries may occur.

Despite the fact that the word "boundaries" literally denotes the polar opposite of what it is used to express, many people use it to characterize unpleasant, rude, or restricting behavior. Boundaries can be defined as constraints that people set on themselves for their own protection. These restrictions can include feelings, wants, and obligations. Their environment has a significant impact on HSPs, and they require boundaries to act as a filter for their behavior.

Limiting how much work you can do helps keep expectations realistic for HSPs who tend to overextend themselves to others.

Many people learn to sacrifice or disregard their demands as a result of their ability to detect subtleties in people's moods and behavior. They genuinely enjoy assisting others and fostering a sense of well-being in those around them in order to keep the peace. If putting others' needs ahead of their own can bring up buried issues, it's time to seek help. According to psychotherapist Carolyn Cole, a large number of HSPs prefer to dwell on their feelings of depletion rather than make others feel bad for disappointing them.

The Power In Saying 'No'

Many highly sensitive people find it difficult to say 'no' without feeling bad because of their finely tuned sensitivity. Regardless, it is critical that people who are extremely sensitive learn to say 'no' when it comes to self-care and building good relationships. Simply allowing ourselves to be overwhelmed, resentful or codependent is not an option.

Many HSPs I have encountered have a lifelong struggle of learning to say 'no' to family members without feeling guilty. However, in order to maintain limits in difficult relationships, it is necessary to first practice by establishing boundaries in everyday situations.

If you are presented with a request, you must first connect with your emotions. Even if you feel compelled to respond immediately, it is critical to always respond in a reflective manner. Look inward and ask yourself, "How does a 'yes' or a 'no' feel in my body?" Gently notice where you feel it and then allow your body to speak for itself.

As you practice noticing and listening to your own needs, it becomes easier to refuse and say 'no' without feeling guilty. When you're aware of how you're feeling, you're better able to identify patterns that no longer serve you. The truth is, when you are asked to provide an answer, you usually know what it is. However, if you do not do what the other person desires, you will be unhappy. Ultimately, sacrificing your own desires benefits no one. Helping someone is a noble and good thing to do, but unless you include yourself in your relationships, you are doing yourself and the other person a disservice.

Declare your response aloud. If the answer is "yes," you may want to place conditions or limits on it. When doing so, keep in mind that others will accept "Yes, as soon as..." rather than "No, I can't..." The following are some examples of boundary setting when saying "yes":

- "I am confident that I can assist you. I won't be able to work this week, but I can help you the following week."
- "That's fantastic; I'll join you. However, there's a chance I'll have to leave early."

When it comes to saying "no," you can be both firm and gentle. When people press you to find a way to meet their needs, they may question your reasons for being unable or unwilling to act. It is completely sufficient if you say "no" without feeling bad about it. Consider using the following statements:

- "That's not going to work for me."
- "I'm sorry, but that's something I can't do right now."
- "It sounds like a lot of fun, but I'm afraid I won't be able to attend."

Appreciate the times when you enforce your boundaries and they are followed. Even if it was a difficult effort, standing up for yourself can have a huge impact. If you truly want to be happy, give yourself love and allow yourself to feel empowered. Be patient and understanding with yourself when you believe you have fallen short.

It is also empowering to express gratitude to those who respect your needs. People who respect your boundaries often go unnoticed, so it's easy to believe they should act in certain ways. When people honor your boundaries, you can respond with simple statements such as "Thank you for understanding," "It was difficult for me to ask for that, so I really appreciate that you..." As a result, it promotes respectful boundaries, increasing the likelihood that the other person will do the same in the future.

Set Small Boundaries First

Stress prevention and management can assist you in reaching your full potential. Now is the time to evaluate your needs and emotions consciously and honestly. When you become aware of your own desires and feelings, you will be able to set firm boundaries. You'll know when you reach your limits based on your thoughts, feelings, and physical experiences. For example, when you are tired, consider what boundaries you must set in order to recharge your energy. When you're hungry, your body sends you subtle cues to eat. Nonetheless, we've become so accustomed to ignoring our bodies' signals and continuing to push ourselves.

Patience will ultimately assist you in sensing and inferring what boundaries you require for yourself. The best way to begin is to take it slow and set small boundaries. There are several occasions when it is appropriate to say you need to leave a gathering or when you should not immediately respond to a text or phone call.

While you can set various boundaries for yourself, such as sticking to a budget or avoiding work after a certain time, you can also start by identifying your own limits. Setting these minor boundaries will give you more confidence to set larger boundaries to reduce tension and worry. The use of gentle "no's" are an effective way to ease into boundary setting. Approaching people politely makes it much easier to turn difficult no's into "not right now." Here are some examples:

- "I am currently very busy, so will there be another opportunity for us to meet in the near future?"
- "Due to a prior commitment, I am unable to attend; however, we may choose another time that is more convenient for me."
- "I enjoy assisting you, but it is stressful when you require immediate assistance. "
- "Would you be able to contact me the day before?"

When you begin to prioritize yourself, using soft "no's is an excellent start. When implementing this strategy, make certain that you are truly committed to making it a reality in the future. If you're unsure how to say 'no', make a suggestion to the other person instead. For instance, you may be asked to participate in a project that is outside of your area of expertise. You may know someone who would be interested in taking on the project, or you may be able to recommend someone to the person who is interested in taking on the job. Of course, you are not required to provide anything to that individual, but it may make saying 'no' easier.

The highly sensitive person may be hesitant to express their desires for fear of being rejected or hurting someone's feelings, which can lead to confusion and misunderstanding. Common motivations for yielding to others' demands include insecurity and a desire to feel accepted. This could be because HSPs have previously felt evaluated for their sensitivity, which influences how HSPs perceive their own insecurities.

Pay attention to being direct as a strategy for forming connections with others based on love and understanding. While doing so, remind yourself of how valuable you are. You may take as much time as you need to make decisions as long as you have considered each option.

Make time for self-care and learn to relax.

We live in a society where people can be reached via text or email, which is why they expect instant responses. An HSP's concentration span can be quite long, especially if there is a lot of new information to process. Most HSPs feel compelled to maintain their hectic lifestyles because, deep down, they want to recharge.

Spend some time thinking about what you want to say 'yes' to instead of rushing into it a new request. When you do receive that request or invitation, take the time to thoroughly examine it before responding. It's fine to say "Let me check my calendar and get back to you later."

Incorporating a daily routine into your life can also help you make better decisions. Make a list of the activities and habits that make you feel replenished. It is possible to stimulate creativity by taking a stroll, doing some light exercise, watching a hilarious movie, or doing nothing at all.

Since you can't pour from an empty cup, taking some time to recharge allows you to be more attentive to your personal and professional needs. It is beneficial to develop the habit of speaking positively about oneself. The importance of scheduling time each week to say 'yes' to only you cannot be overstated.

Acknowledging and accepting who you are rather than trying to control or repress aspects of your personality that define you as "you" will allow you to begin living life on your own terms. Ultimately, high sensitivity is a treasure. You will feel empowered once you accept your intrinsic value simply for being you. Don't let the false belief that limits are bad deter you from using them; instead, think of them as a way to protect your energy, peace of mind, and well-being. Limiting yourself in a loving way leads to deeper connections and allows you to enjoy all of your unique talents.

Boundary Setting Exercise

The following exercise will help you to establish and implement your most important boundaries to achieve a healthier sense of self.

When we talk about identifying "rights", we are acknowledging and addressing our core values. Take some time to think through each step and get acquainted with what is most important to you.

1. Identify Your Rights

If you don't know your boundaries, it's impossible to set healthy ones. Spend some time contemplating and journaling your rights. You should take into account all of your connections and situations in life and your rights in each one. A few examples of your rights are the freedom of self-expression as well as the ability to feel comfortable in the company of your partner, both physically and emotionally. More common examples include:

- I have the right to express my thoughts and emotions without fear of judgment
- I have the right to say 'no' without feeling guilty
- I have the right to prioritize my self-care before accepting requests from others

Personal Rights:

_____

_____

_____

You may have rights at work, such as not being subjected to discrimination or being contacted after hours.

Workplace Rights:

_____

_____

_____

If you have a family, you may feel entitled to put your own needs ahead of the needs of others.

Family Rights:

_____

_____

_____

By laying out your rights, you'll be able to discover the areas of your life where your boundaries are weak and need to be reinforced.

2. State Your Core Values

To set effective boundaries, we must first understand our personal values, which form the basis of our borders. Shared interests or working toward joint goals may be among the values you hold close in your relationship.

Working towards a healthy work-life balance or engaging in a positive business culture may be among your professional values. Family values may include spending time together in a meaningful way or even reducing the amount of time you spend together.

Write a list of your top five essential values, and then cut the list down to three or four. This will allow you to decide what to accept or tolerate in any particular situation, along with, what you won't.

My Core Values include the following:
1.
2.
3.
4.
5.

3. Define Your Boundaries

Now it's time to translate your core values into boundaries now that you've identified them. For each core value, ask yourself the three following questions:

- What will I allow?
- What am I willing to tolerate?
- What will I not allow?

Value 1: _____

I will allow…

_____

I will tolerate…

_____

I will <u>not</u> allow …

_____

Value 2: _____

I will allow…

_____

I will tolerate…

_____

I will <u>not</u> allow …

_____

Value 3: _____

I will allow…

_____

I will tolerate…

_____

I will <u>not</u> allow …

_____

Make a note of your answers for future reference and use this to re-enforce your boundaries when the situation arises.

4. Communicate Your Limits

When you're clear about your expectations, the other person knows what to expect from you. To some degree, we've all crossed the line with one another due to the fact that everyone has their own set of rules and expectations. It's generally an accident, therefore making someone aware of your limits will assist them in avoiding doing so again.

Chapter 8. Home Organization for the Highly Sensitive

Minimalism, simplification, and clutter removal are critical for highly sensitive people. A cluttered environment with too many things can make anyone feel distressed. But this is especially true for a highly sensitive individual. Due to clutter, a highly sensitive person will be bombarded with an excess of external stimuli, causing sensory overload and anxiety. A crowded environment gives your eyes and mind fewer opportunities to rest. It's simply too much to look at and process. Highly sensitive people find it difficult to relax or rest because their senses are overstimulated by the disorder.

Consider an environment with few distractions, uncluttered surfaces, and plenty of breathing room. Such a setting promotes feelings of openness and relaxation. Your eyes and mind can find peace in an uncluttered room with clean surfaces. Because HSPs are more sensitive to their surroundings than the ordinary person, minimalism may appeal to HSPs who do better with fewer stimuli in their environment. Minimalism enables highly sensitive people to create the environment in which they truly need to rest, relax, and rejuvenate. This is especially true after being exposed to the world and its sensory overload all day.

Minimalism itself is not a new concept. In fact, you practice minimalism every time you clean up your workspace and get rid of unnecessary clutter. You also put it into practice by taking a moment to reflect before making a purchase. Extreme levels of loudness, intense activity, and an overwhelming number of options quickly deplete HSPs' energy reserves. Due to the fact that minimalism minimizes the amount of material you have, it is possible to eliminate this stream of overwhelming thoughts. Every person in our culture is constantly on the lookout for something bigger, better, newer, and faster. The quest for 'more' seems to have no end in sight.

A common result of this is that HSPs begin to feel as though they do not belong in this culture. They believe they are forced to choose between trying to fit into a fast-paced world that exhausts them fully or distancing themselves from social chances or occupations that are too demanding, risking feeling isolated and lonely as a result of their decision.

Minimalism assists HSPs in creating an environment and plan in which they can thrive. If you recognize your limits as a highly sensitive person, you can use minimalism ideals to free yourself from the clutter - the hobbies, relationships, and things that make you worse - so you can make room for more peace. Even in this high consumption culture, you can live a life that is true to yourself.

Minimalism forces you to consider questions such as:

- What do I really need?
- What am I going to do with my life?
- What are my priorities?

This is a process that gradually reveals the significance of your existence. When you realize what's important to you, letting go becomes much easier. After some thought, most HSPs will realize that a peaceful and soothing home is more important to them than a large number of possessions. Of course, the removal of your space is frequently the first step that most HSPs take to begin their minimalism journey.

An atmosphere that reflects your ideals and creates quiet and relaxing feelings is a welcome respite from the chaos of the outside world. When HSPs return home, they require a retreat to restore their sensitive souls. Minimalism helps to clear the clutter and, at the end of the day, creates a relaxing environment.

Many HSPs can feel befuddled and alone at times. However, if you begin to consider the large culture that feeds on simplicity and a slower pace of life, you discover you are not alone. HSPs may be a quieter lot, but their role in society is critical in advancing cultural standards and advocating for a simpler way of life.

After experiencing the benefits of downgrading your physical environment, you will most likely be inspired to apply minimalism to every aspect of your life. As previously discussed, you can begin to thrive if you say 'yes' to fewer tasks and obligations, and focusing more on things that genuinely reflect your own beliefs. In short, minimalism contributes to the creation of an environment and a way of life that allow you to rest, unwind, and recharge after being exposed to the sensory overload of the world all day.

Since we are constantly looking for ways to improve culture through excess, this frequently gives HSP the impression that they only have two choices. They can either participate fully in the world by sharing their talents or they can choose to remove themselves from culture. They can choose not to attend social gatherings or decide not to pursue their career because their role required them to remain in situations that were not beneficial to them. Either is an option, but both have consequences for a person's health and well-being.

When highly sensitive people choose to participate fully in the world – as if they are not physically exhausted at work every day – they are most likely engaging in unhealthy routines. Perfectionism can be used to shield themselves from criticism since HSPs tend to take criticism hard. Or they may turn to addiction (like food or alcohol) to help soften the acute ache of raw feelings and being overwhelmed with information. They run the risk of feeling isolated if they decide to withdraw completely from the world.

However, engaging in minimalism, or "essentialism" as it is sometimes known, can help provide a framework for extremely sensitive people to navigate to the middle. Life should not be reduced to either feeling overfed or undernourished. We simply need to figure out what is important to us and be courageous enough to speak our truth.

Optimize Your Home Organization as an HSP

If you have a high level of sensitivity, having a safe place to retreat after stressful activities is critical. That is why this section is included to be a guide for establishing a home environment that functions as a sanctuary.

This section will cover every room in the house with ideas and tactics for creating a home that is suitable for living with high sensitivities. Every HSP understands the importance of creating a quiet environment. The following room-by-room hacks are presented for optimal rest and relaxation.

Bedroom:

For many people who are sensitive, the bedroom is the safest place to be. Therefore, if you suffer from nighttime anxiety, it is critical that your bedroom is designed to meet your specific requirements. To create a sleeping sanctuary, employ the following strategies:

- Install blackout curtains to reduce morning sunlight and create a gloomy, sleepy environment. Because light exposure affects sleep quality, it is necessary for extremely sensitive people, particularly those with light sensitivity, to eliminate as much light as possible while sleeping.

- Invest in high-quality linens to improve your sleep. Saving money on bed frames and other bedroom furnishings is perfectly acceptable, but investing in high-quality bedding and pillows can have a major impact on your ability to relax.

- Clutter can be hidden under the bed with storage baskets and containers. Studies show that having an organized bedroom reduces stress and improves sleep.

- If you live in an apartment, it is best to avoid working in your bedroom if you want to break the subconscious association between sleep and stressful work. Instead of having an open wall between your bedroom and the rest of the apartment, consider installing an opaque curtain to separate work from play.

- Incorporate soothing, neutral tones into your bedroom's color scheme. Continue to use gray, cream, or tan as the foundation color, with a blue or green accent for a splash of color that evokes peaceful and peaceful feelings.

- Remove TVs and other screens, including phones, to avoid blue light penetration and to disrupt the sleep cycle.

These suggestions not only improve the aesthetics of your bedroom, but they also promote a more relaxing environment.

The Living Room

For many people, the living room is the most popular room in the house. Whether you spend your evenings watching television or curling up with a good book in your favorite chair, the ambiance in your living room is essential if you are a highly sensitive person.

Create the ideal living room by incorporating the following ideas:

- Make your couch and sleeves cozier by adding soft throw pillows and blankets. Make an effort to avoid textiles such as nylon and polyester.

- Consider the flow of the room. Use feng shui principles to direct the flow of energy between the various pieces of furniture in the room. The right setup can drastically reduce your stress levels.

- Always have a vase of fresh flowers on hand. Having a bouquet or a potted plant around increases the release of dopamine, the hormone that makes you feel good.

- Keep pictures of relatives and friends around. Having family photos nearby can help HSPs feel more connected to their relatives. Family faces also provide the sense of continuity that many sensitive people seek.

- To make your night cozy, place white candles on fireplaces, side tables, or coffee tables. Avoid using particularly fragrant candles because the aroma can be overwhelming for those who are sensitive to strong odors.

Kitchen

When living with high sensitivity, it is critical to plan your kitchen for maximum utility and organization, regardless of whether you enjoy cooking or prefer takeout. The following strategies can assist you in maintaining a peaceful and functioning kitchen:

- Organize your drawers and shelves using dividers and organizers. Keeping everything in order is crucial for HSPs since they thrive on order and harmony.

- Keep the kitchen smelling fresh by placing an air purifier near garbage cans to remove aromas. Those with a keen sense of smell enjoy breathing in fresh air.

- Replace bright LED lights with dimmer controls. Total lighting management will make a difference in the atmosphere of the kitchen.

- Place sound-absorbing cushions in all cupboards and drawers. The sound of a slamming drawer can be deafening to those with high acoustic sensitivity.

- For the quietest cooking area, invest in ultra-quiet equipment. Sound-sensitive equipment (everything from coolers to blenders) will be a relief for any HSP who is affected by loud or unexpected sounds.

Bathroom

Whether your bathroom is small and cramped or a sprawling luxury spa, any bathroom can be customized to meet the needs of an HSP.

- Keep essential oils near the bath to incorporate aromatherapy into your evening bubble baths. Add a few drops of essential oils to your bathroom-- the hot water activates the aroma and produces a calming effect.

- Play soft music with a waterproof speaker while working or relaxing in a hot bubble bath. Listening to music modifies the working of the brain to improve concentration and lessen anxiety.

- Invest in spa-quality towels and bathrobes. Many people who are allergic to certain materials are especially sensitive, and a low-quality material, such as polyester, can cause skin irritation. Towels made of bamboo, Egyptian, or pure cotton have the best feel.

- If you're renting an apartment, it's especially important to have a new shower head. Showering with a rain shower head is more calming since it simulates the sound and feel of rain. A new shower head is simple to install and portable when you move.

Home Office

A well-organized workplace environment is essential for those who do their business from home. People who are more sensitive to noise and distraction will need to make some adjustments in order to create a productive working environment.

- Promote proper posture by using an ergonomic office chair, lumbar support cushions and coated mouse pads for the wrist. A standing desk is another excellent option for improved posture and wellness.

- Purchase noise-cancelling headphones to reduce distractions and provide a sense of seclusion while at home. These are especially effective for HSPs who are sensitive to sound.

- Maintain a calendar to track daily events such as work, mental health, self-care and diet plans. This daily practice not only provides HSPs with the consistency they seek, but also allows greater awareness of emotion, mental health, and memory.

- Reduce artificial light. To keep your energy levels up throughout the day, opt for natural light with pure window drapes. Sunshine has numerous health benefits, including improved mental wellness, reduced stress, and even improved sleep.

- Keep a fidget cube at your workstation to redirect stored energy during meetings, performances, and brainstorming sessions. This aids many HSPs in avoiding additional harmful habits such as nail-biting.

Soothing activities for HSPs at Homes

While being at home is frequently the most calming environment for highly sensitive people, no one wants to be at home for an extended period of time. Unfortunately, there are a few situations in which people must stay at home for long periods like quarantine lockdowns, snow days or sick days.

If you find yourself in a situation like this and are looking for suggestions on how to keep yourself occupied, comfortable, and quiet, consider the following:

Gardening: To feed your creative side and relieve stress, tend to patio plants or arrange flowers. Plant and floral exposure has been shown to lower stress hormones.

Mind teasers: Finish a puzzle or crossword puzzle to keep your mind focused and productive. Some people who are extremely sensitive are easily distracted. Maintain these habits to improve cognitive stimulation.

Self-care: Spend some time on yourself and indulge in some self-pampering activities like taking bubble baths, applying masks, and eating ice cream. For many HSPs, taking time to relax helps alleviate the "information overload" feeling that follows a long day.

Meditation: Every few hours, devote 15-20 minutes to a soothing activity such as journaling, yoga, reading, or meditation. Peace and silence are the ultimate tools for those who are hypersensitive.

Cooking: Experiment with new recipes or try to create your own dish in the kitchen. It's common for HSPs to be highly creative, so finding a way to put that creativity to good use can be gratifying.

Alone time: Consider setting aside some quiet time for yourself if you share a home. Individuals with high emotional sensitivity, such as introverts, prefer to spend time alone to recharge and relax.

Decluttering: Every day, set aside ten minutes to clean up your surroundings. You can try the KonMari method for added stress relief. A clean, tidy environment, especially when indoors, is essential for good mental health.

Connect through video chat: You can use FaceTime, Skype, or Google Hangouts to contact old friends. Intimate relationships and meaningful conversations are essential for people with high sensitivity, so make time to interact with your friends when you're at home.

Apartment Organization for the Highly Sensitive

As a highly sensitive individual, there are numerous other ways to adapt apartment living to meet your needs.

- Create an area for yoga or meditation. When you live in an apartment complex, you may also have access to a community gym, walkways, or outdoor space that can be used for physical activity. Physical activity is beneficial to HSPs who are under stress.

- Use emotional support animals or dog therapy. Look for animal-friendly rentals that offer discounts to ESA-enrolled pets.

- Make decisions based on your requirements. If you are afraid of heights, look for apartments that do not have balconies or shades that cover patio doors.

- Take into account the community's environment. For HSPs who are sensitive to noise, living on the top floor can help to reduce the sound of their upper-floor neighbors. A complex primarily populated by university students, for example, may indicate parties and late-night loud music.

Maintaining a peaceful and uncluttered mind is made easier by living in a quiet and orderly surroundings. By adhering to the principles of minimalism, highly sensitive people can create an environment in which they can truly rest, relax, and rejuvenate. This is especially true after being exposed to the rest of the day to the outside world with all its sensory stimuli.

Chapter 9. Continued Growth as an HSP

Why do you think successful people have certain characteristics? It's not difficult to be envious of their problem solving skills and inventiveness. Or perhaps their emotional intelligence and ability to engage with people impress you. These are just a few of the characteristics that characterize approximately 20% of the population of highly sensitive people.

As an HSP, you are fully aware there are disadvantages to this inherent trait, however, with enough forethought and intention, you can use your high sensitivity as your strongest strength. Highly sensitive people make excellent leaders and are consistently ranked as top performers. HSPs are also well-regarded by managers and admired for their dedication, even if they occasionally irritate their coworkers.

Fortunately, society's perception of this sensitivity is changing, thanks in part to a growing acceptance of neurodiversity—the belief that neurological changes are normal in people.

So why do I bring this up?

Because now is the time to make use of your highly sensitive abilities. Your attention to detail, sense of structure, and sense of organization are among your strongest abilities. Your familiarity with dealing with large amounts of information has given you the ability to devise plans and solutions for a variety of situations quickly.

Strength Assessment Exercise

The purpose of this exercise is to help you become more acquainted with your unique gifts and locate opportunities to put them to use.

For this exercise, select which of the following highly sensitive gifts you most identify with. Then, for each instance, identify how they were applied and where you may have neglected to use them.

Personal strengths:

☐ I am aware of what's going on in the hearts, minds and lives of those I care about most.
☐ I have a natural ability to make others feel heard and understood.
☐ I have a strong sense of connection to the people and places around me, as well as the reason I was put on this earth.
☐ I am often deeply spiritual and feel connected to nature and animals.

In what specific instances did I apply these gift at home, with my family or with friends?

_____

_____

_____

Were there any situations where I could have put my skills to better use?

_____

_____

Workplace:

☐ My self-awareness is unmatched.
☐ I am a brilliant critical thinker.
☐ I am diplomatic when it matters most.
☐ I am skilled at spotting opportunities for innovation.
☐ I am constantly learning and growing.
☐ I am a pillar of integrity.
☐ I create a harmonious work environment.
☐ I focus on the big picture.
☐ I impress others with my thoroughness.

☐ I have strong intuition.
☐ I have a pulse on team morale.
☐ I am capable of integrating and managing large amounts of information.

In what specific instances have I applied my gifts at work?

_____

_____

Were there any situations where I could have put my skills to better use?

_____

_____

Positive Affirmations

As a highly sensitive individual, there will undoubtedly be moments where overstimulation becomes too difficult to bare. To help you take stock of yourself when this happens, here are a few affirmations you can use whenever you want. You can use them to start your day with a positive thought or implement them in a moment when you're feeling overwhelmed.

Try implementing any of the following statements:

- I'm going to listen to what my body has to say. I will stick to a balanced diet. I will engage in self care activities to conquer my addictions and maintain a physical, emotional, and spiritual balance.

- I don't have to feel bad about saying no to others. It's okay to set limits to protect my time, health, and energy.

- My heightened emotional awareness serves as both a blessing and a strength. I welcome the unique features and abilities that come with it.

- I make a commitment to respect my boundaries and be gentle with myself as I learn what it takes to fully appreciate my unique talents. I'm going to thank myself every day.

- I am a powerful person. I have high hopes. I have the power to rid my body of any tension and negativity. I make it a priority to take care of my mental, emotional, and spiritual well-being.

- I'm going to be kind, loving, and considerate to myself, considering my own interests before committing to others.

- My body has the ability to provide me with information about people, places, and circumstances. As a result, I pay great attention and place a lot of trust in my gut.

- I'm going to be aware of my limitations and set aside time to recharge. I'll let people who can help me know what I need. I'm not going to try to hide my ability in any way.

- I promise to be open and honest, and I'll make it clear how much power I have. As a sensitive and kind individual, it makes me happy to be who I am.

- I will take self-care measures in my professional life to protect my sensitivity. In my spare time, I intend to play and rest to replenish my energy stores.

- I deserve to be in a committed relationship with someone who makes me feel loved and safe. As a human being, I have a right to express myself and my true needs. It's important to keep my sensitivity in mind. I'm entitled to be taken seriously.

- I'm going to value myself and commit to being around people who value me. My goal is to make a difference in my own life and the lives of others by utilizing my high level of sensitivity.

- I'll go with what my instincts tell me. To express my full spectrum of sensitivity and remain whole, I will endeavor to maintain a sense of balance in my intuition and other areas of my life.

Conclusion

I want to take this opportunity to congratulate you on completing this book. I understand that some of the information may have been challenging to you, and that many of the events depicted may have been all too familiar. I hope you've received a greater appreciation for your strengths as a highly sensitive person and how to better manage your symptoms.

Throughout this book, you've learned how to improve your life as an HSP and how to be an assertive individual in an overstimulating world. Together we explored the traits of hypersensitivity and the adult ramifications of childhood neglect. You were given a brief self-assessment quiz to determine if you are a highly sensitive person. In chapter two you learned techniques for mastering emotional regulation and how to identify and manage unpleasant emotions.

The third chapter showed you how to deal with overstimulation and how to manage the common emotional concerns connected with guilt and shame that plague HSPs. In chapter four, you learned the important components of effective communication to enhance your assertiveness and discovered practical steps on how to accept your point of view, manage your concerns, and be more self-confident. We also examined ways to be successful in the workplace while still controlling your sensitivities. You learned how to deal with common workplace concerns such as excessive analysis and how to cope with an overstimulating environment. In addition, you learned how to maximize your abilities and avoid career stagnation as an HSP.

In chapter six, we delved deeper into the personal side of things by providing techniques for resolving typical relationship conflicts and partner discontent. You gained an understanding of how to recognize and balance HSP characteristics in a relationship in order to avoid conflict and distress.

You discovered how to set personal boundaries as an HSP and were taught practical steps to saying "no". You learned how limiting yourself may result in deeper connections and the capacity to completely express all of your unique talents and abilities.

You also learned the powerful effect of minimalism in chapter eight. I discussed how to optimize your home organization by learning the best room-by-room techniques for maximizing your space and soothing your sensitivities. In the final chapter, you learned how to take stock in your natural gifts and were provided power affirmations to incorporate into you life for greater self esteem.

Now that you have finished this book, I want to leave you with this very important thought:

We must first acknowledge all of the wonderful features that come with having highly sensitive tendencies in ourselves before we can begin to embrace them. Highly sensitive people possess amazing characteristics that allow them to live a more fulfilling life, improve the lives of others, and contribute to the betterment of the world. The first step toward making peace with your sensitivity is to learn to accept your own personal qualities. It is only when we allow ourselves to be curiously aware of our feelings that we are able to more thoughtfully process and express them.

I wish you the best of luck on your path to becoming the most complete version of yourself!

References

Acevedo, B. (2014, July 1). The Highly Sensitive Brain: an FMRI Study Of Sensory Processing Sensitivity And Response To Others' Emotions. PubMed Central (PMC). https://www.ncbi.nlm.nih.gov/pmc/articles/PMC4086365/.

Aron, E.N. The Highly Sensitive Person: How to Thrive When the World Overwhelms You. New York: Birch Lane Press, 1996.

Gottman, John. The Seven Principles for Making Marriage Work. Orion, 2000.

Made in the USA
Columbia, SC
09 November 2024

46069657R00059